The Daily Chase

In Hot Pursuit of His Presence

Tommy Tenney

Distributed by
Destiny Image₀ Publishers, Inc.
P.O. Box 310
Shippensburg, PA 17257-0310

ISBN 0-7684-2061-X

First Printing: 2002   Second Printing: 2003

For Worldwide Distribution
Printed in the U.S.A.

This book and all other Destiny Image, Revival Press, MercyPlace, Fresh Bread, Destiny Image Fiction, and Treasure House books are available at Christian bookstores and distributors worldwide.

For a U.S. bookstore nearest you, call **1-800-722-6774**.
For more information on foreign distributors, call **717-532-3040**.
Or reach us on the Internet: **www.destinyimage.com**

Endorsements

Tommy Tenney takes us back to the ancient landmarks of biblical truth. These powerful, practical, and essential revelations will aid the spiritual pilgrim in his quest to know God and His ways.

David Ravenhill
Teacher and Author

For those who have sought God and found Him, this book uncovers biblical "power points" that will help them lay aside the weights and care of this world and find freedom in Christ.

Vinson Synan
Dean of the School of Divinity
Regent University

This is a powerful book! Tommy has a unique gift for finding the real truth in Scripture and illuminating it for the rest of us.

Mike Bickle
Director, International House of Prayer
Kansas City, Missouri

As a gatekeeper, Tenney props the door open, allowing us to glimpse the glory of God, and challenges us to experience this in our own lives and communities by completely and totally abandoning ourselves to worshiping God.

Pastor Dutch Sheets
Colorado Springs, Colorado

I totally identify with Tommy Tenney's passionate pursuit of the sustained manifest presence of the Lord Jesus. His writings echo the deepest, desperate cries of my own heart.

Joy Dawson
International Bible Teacher and Author

Tommy Tenney shares his single-minded pursuit with the honesty of a disciple who is caught at last by His holy presence.

Jane Hansen
President, Aglow International

Tommy holds no punches as he pleads with us to become desperate and determined in our pursuit of God.

Ted Haggard
Senior Pastor, New Life Church
Colorado Springs, Colorado

Tommy Tenney is inspiring a whole new generation to go from being pew-sitters to God chasers. The Body of Christ has desperately needed someone to inspire them to follow after God with all their heart.

Ron Luce
President, Teen Mania Ministries

Do you want to be free, happy, fulfilled, and confident that you are exactly where God wants you to be? I know of no better starting point than reading the works of Tommy Tenney.

C. Peter Wagner
Chancellor, Wagner Leadership Institute

Contents

Contents

Introduction

There is a vast difference between having an encounter with God and having a relationship with Him. It's like the difference between a sprint and a marathon. Anyone can start a marathon—but the honor goes to those who finish and finish well.

A marathon is more than just a Sunday morning "fun run." It requires dedication, determination, and discipline. It means staying the course—running even when you'd rather give up and collapse. Stamina and direction can be more important than speed.

This book is dedicated to people who are more than Sunday morning sprinters. They understand that a relationship with God is a Daily Chase.

May this devotional be fuel for those dedicated God chasers who do not simply desire to run, but to finish the race and finish well.

This book is more than a Sunday morning "fun run." This is a red lights flashing, sirens blaring, "in-hot-pursuit" book!

Read and Run!

Tommy Tenney
Author, GodChaser

The Hammer Blows of Life Will Bend Us Godward If...

oo many of us just want to be pre-formed or pre-cast in a quick and easy "one-two-three revival formula." I can't give that to you. However, I can tell you that your wings of worship can be created only one way. They must be beaten into the proper position and the proper image. *The hammer blows of life will bend us "Godward" if our responses to life's challenges are right.* Sometimes we respond wrongly to what life sends us; then the adversity beats us out of position. *Instead of becoming "better" we become "bitter."* This means that our wings of worship will not be where they are supposed to be; they will be in the right place but in the wrong position—in church but with a wrong attitude.

God intends for the hammer blows of life to move your wings of worship into position so as to create one who "in all things gives thanks." (See 1 Thessalonians 5:18.) The apostle Paul knew about this. He wrote, "For to me to live is Christ, and to die is gain" (Phil. 1:21). He wrote these words while under Roman house arrest and awaiting the verdict of Caesar. Paul could declare, "Every time you hit me, all it does is teach me how to worship!" *His visit to the third heaven came while being stoned at Lystra!* Anybody want to go there now?

When the worshipers around the mercy seat come into *their* position, God can move into *His* position and occupy the middle ground between them.

The beaten gold cherubim of the ark of the covenant were only a poor earthly representation of the heavenly reality. Moses saw the pattern on the mount when he peeked into Heaven and saw the throne room in a vision. He was instructed to recreate that heavenly vision, and it is as if the closest he could come on earth was to create solid gold cherubim that only had two wings. The seraphim surrounding God's true heavenly throne have six wings.

The mercy seat on the ark was only a representation of God's true throne in the third heaven. The throne in the heavenlies isn't situated on a two-dimensional plane, so it can't be described solely with width and height measurements. The ark of the covenant featured two cherubim mounted on the flat cover of the ark. In contrast, the Scriptures describe the true throne of God as multidimensional and surrounded by worshipers on all sides, much like a pearl suspended in glass or the sun in the middle of our solar system. The Bible says there are six-winged seraphim on both sides of the throne and more above and beneath as well. These worshiping seraphim cover their faces with two wings while covering their feet with two more wings, and flying with the third pair. (See Isaiah 6:2.)

Even though the cherubim on the ark amounted to a "cheap earthly imitation" of the heavenly reality, there is still so much mystique about the ark that Hollywood producers made millions of dollars simply by talking about the "lost ark" in an adventure film.

When will the Church realize that God isn't looking for the lost ark; He knows where that is. *He is looking for "the lost worshipers"* so He can replace the lost glory in the earth.

The "mercy seat" rarely if ever appears in the midst of religious pomp and circumstance. Under the covenant of Christ's blood, it only comes between two or more living sacrifices. Paul and Silas were far from the ornate temple and the synagogues of Jerusalem and Israel; they were bloodied and battered with their feet locked in stocks deep in a Philippian jail cell. Yet at their darkest hour, these men began to pray and sing to the Lord in worship and adoration. All they did was bring together their battered wings of worship and the glory of God descended from Heaven to join them there. Their worship created the "mercy seat" for God to come and sit between them—*even in jail.*

You may be "in jail" even as you read these words. Perhaps the circumstances of life have locked you up and thrown away the key. There is a way of escape. *"Worship" a hole in the heavenlies.* God will come down. He promised. What He did for Paul and Silas He will do for you.

The sudden weight of His coming rocked the earth and shook the foundations of their prison. Not only did the weight of God's presence free His worshipers, but it also opened every door and freed every prisoner in the vicinity! *Our worship can set captives free.* God's visitation in power led to the salvation of the same jailer who had put the stocks on the feet of Paul and Silas.

Don't fear adversity! The cherubim were formed of beaten gold. And worshipers formed of fire-purified gold and beaten through adversity and trials in our day, refract the light of God's glory in the house a lot better than quickie pre-cast versions. Every hammer indentation, every pick and awl mark, and every crease of transformation under pressure of pounding is another reflector for the multifaceted glory of God.

When we worship in spirit and in truth, the glory of God will come. What we will experience at that point is simply a precursor of what will happen on that great day when the King of Glory personally returns to the earth for the second time. The first time He came, He carried His glory lightly because He walked in humility. He tiptoed through our world so He would not disturb His creation, much as an adult tiptoes through a child's playroom to avoid breaking the toys.

The next time Jesus appears, He will be astride a horse and will come in unrestrained power and authority to repossess the entire house. When His feet touch the top of the Mount of Olives, His *kabod*, His weighty glory, will be so great that the Mount of Olives will literally split in two. The eastern gate will suddenly open to allow His "real" triumphant entry. *The first was just the rehearsal.* **Next time He will be in costume!** And every knee will bow and every tongue will confess that Jesus Christ is Lord.

Tommy Tenney – *God's Favorite House*

The Enemy Wants to Wear You Out

*D*aniel the prophet said that in the end times, the anti-Christ would "*wear out* the saints of the Most High...." (Dan. 7:25b). The spirit of anti-Christ is at work in the world right now, and it comes against us in the form of little things that keep weighing on us. They drain our creative energies and work to rob us of spiritual integrity unit by unit. These things don't quite qualify as sin—they are just unnecessary weights. The power to run, the power to endure, and the power to stay focused rests with our ability to unload those encumbering, entangling weights. It begins with the wisdom of knowing what to take on and what to let go.

Children need to learn two principles when they are young. First, they need to learn the principle of discipline: Life is not doing what you want to do; it is doing what you ought to do. Secondly, they should learn the principle of priorities: Your relationship with God is the single most important relationship in your life. Second is family; and third is your ministry and calling. We must encourage them—and ourselves—to set godly priorities and discipline themselves to follow them.

Improper priorities can quickly overload us with duties, commitments, and projects that lead far from where we belong. The greatest danger is that "the temporal" will crowd out "the eternal."

Very few church problems are based on eternal issues. The problems usually stem from disagreements about minor "temporal" or non-eternal things such as: "my money," "my piano," "my church," "my rights...." Very few church meetings turn contentious over questions of false doctrine, but countless church congregations have split after disagreeing about minor money disbursement decisions, church decorations, and even the placement of coat racks in the foyer!

We tend to be more "problem conscious" than "power conscious." Perhaps this is why Jesus instructed His disciples on one occasion to come aside or come apart for a while. (See Mark 6:31.) If you don't "come apart for a little while," then you might "fall apart for a long while." Jesus set the example for us by taking time to "unload" in the presence of His Father.

Satan has made it **his priority** *to keep the saints of God from* **their priorities**. He does his best to keep us so bogged down in "things" that we forget to spend time with God. As a result, we are driven by debt, fear, and loneliness. Pharaoh and the taskmasters of Egypt attempted to wear out the children of Israel; in our day, the enemy increases our "Egyptian" responsibilities hoping to do the same thing. We must learn and apply the principles of "unloading" so we can decrease the enemy's ability to overload us. If you don't unload, you will definitely overload (and maybe even blow a fuse!).

T.F. Tenney and Tommy Tenney – *Secret Sources of Power*

Some Things Are Too Big to Carry Alone

*T*ucked away in the mental treasure vaults of every parent and grandparent are memories of little toddlers staggering along under impossible loads as they "helped" various adults in the family carry items of furniture, bulging grocery bags, or overstuffed suitcases prepared for a Christmas holiday at Grandma's house.

It is obvious to us that little children can't carry such loads all by themselves. Frankly, these little "helpers" are usually more nuisance than assistance, but no one really cares. I am always amused when my youngest daughter, Andrea, runs ahead to grab the largest bag of groceries she can find after a trip to the grocery store. The result is predictable. No matter how hard she grunts, groans, or contorts her face, that thing won't budge The truth is the same for both toddlers and adults: *There are some things that are just too big to carry alone.*

Revival is lot a like that. We often run ahead of God and try to carry revival into our churches and cities all by ourselves, thinking our efforts, gifts, and programs can carry the day. Yet no matter how much we grunt, groan, shout, or contort our faces, nothing seems to move.

It all brings me back to the "mercy seat" on the ark of the covenant in the Old Testament. To me, the mercy seat represents my personal passion and dream to see the weighty glory of God dwell among us today like it did back in David's day. I long to see the blue flame of God's presence continually hover among us just as it once hovered between the outstretched wings of the two golden cherubim above the mercy seat.

The mercy seat on the ark of the covenant was just a model of things in Heaven. It was merely a poor earthly representation of glorious heavenly reality because no piece of furniture could ever duplicate the reality of the heavenly scene Moses saw on the mount. Yet there was something that was so inviting about the mercy seat that for some reason God chose to dwell there.

God could have designed the mercy seat and the ark in any number of ways, but I find it interesting that He chose to design it in such a way that one person would not be able to carry it. The ark of the covenant, the earthly dwelling place for heavenly glory, was just too big to be carried alone.

I dream of the day when the tangible glory of God invades our cities. However, just as the ark could never be borne upon a single set of shoulders, *nothing that I could ever do alone* will ever be sufficient to make that dream a reality. That task requires many committed, consecrated individuals who are willing to "grab the poles" and walk *together* to help carry the presence of God into their homes, churches, and cities.

Do you feel like you are carrying a load that is too much for one person to bear? Perhaps the answer lies not in finding others to help you bear your burdens, but in laying down your burdens so you can lift up Jesus' name. The only way the Levites could carry the ark was to put down whatever else they had been carrying to pick up the ark. They had to walk in unity. Just as God was in the midst or middle of the cherubim, He was also in the middle of the four men—the ark bearers. God always dwells in the middle of unity.

Carrying the ark wasn't the sort of job that brought fame or the fortunes of men to those who did it. We find no record of an "ark-carrier's hall of fame." We don't even know the names of most of the selfless individuals who served in this critical capacity. Yet without them, how many battles would have been lost? How might history have been altered if they were absent? One thing we know: If the ark was carried, *they did it together.*

The Job of Unloading Is in Your Portfolio, Not God's!

Many times these people will say, "I've asked God to take it away and He just won't." You could tell them the truth and say, "No, God said for *you* to do it. The Scripture says, '...let *us* lay aside every weight' (Heb. 12:1a NKJV). The job is in your portfolio, not God's." However, don't be surprised if they reply, "I've tried that. I just can't...."

God would not tell us to "lay aside" something if we were not fully capable of doing it. It is not that we *cannot*; it is that we *will not*. We have established habits and imposed things upon ourselves that have nothing to do with the gospel.

Balanced priorities are essential. Some of us tend to become consumed with the work of God while actually neglecting our *relationship* with Him. We get so busy doing the things of God that we sacrifice our walk with God. No one was more dedicated to do the will of God than His Son Jesus. Yet, even though the whole world was lost in darkness, the Bible tells us that Jesus "came apart to rest" or went away from the crowds to be alone for a time. (See Matthew 14:23, Mark 6:31-32, and Mark 6:47 to name just a few.) We need to follow His example, especially when a problem or situation threatens to consume our lives.

It is significant that the first administrative decision of the New Testament church leadership was that the apostles, or those in the "feeding and leading" ministry, were to give themselves to prayer and the Word. They assigned someone else to provide daily care for the widows. The apostles made sure it was done, by delegating the work so it wouldn't become a weight that hindered the propagation of the gospel message to the world.

We can be sure pressure will come at times, but we always face the same choice: pressure or priorities? *You will never come into a dimension of God's power until you learn how to prioritize and unload.* Many things in life will come along to deter you from your goal or slow your progress. Nevertheless, God's thermometer stays fixed; the labels on His bottles don't change with circumstances. He is "the same yesterday, today, and forever" (Heb. 13:8 NKJV). His prescription for health in good times and hard times hasn't changed: "Therefore I exhort first of all that supplications, prayers, intercessions, and giving of thanks be made for all men" (1 Tim. 2:1 NKJV).

The most popular excuse you hear is, "I just don't have time." Yet all of us are given the same number of hours each day. Each of us has 1,440 minutes to "spend" each day. We decide how to use the 86,400 seconds per day, and our management of that time makes all the difference. Some things must be set aside for later, and some things must be unloaded altogether.

T.F. Tenney and Tommy Tenney – *Secret Sources of Power*

If You're Hurting... Heaven Is Close

*H*ave you broken anything recently? Or perhaps had something broken? It seems we're always breaking things. Sometimes we break something when we're actually trying to fix it. A carpenter once broke a water pipe at our house and had to remove part of a wall to repair it. It was a big mess!

When I was a small boy, I constantly tinkered with things to find out how they worked. Usually I could put them back together, but on one occasion I wasn't so fortunate. My mom and dad had a wind-up alarm clock—you've seen them; they're the kind with the two bright brass bells on top. I was fascinated with how the clapper rang the bells. Being inquisitive, I dismantled the alarm clock to figure out how it rang. Once the clock was taken apart, it was apparent how the mechanics of the alarm worked—but the challenge was to put it all back together again. Visions of "Humpty Dumpty" began to flow through my head. "All the King's horses and all the king's men"—including little Tommy Tenney—couldn't put Mom's alarm clock back together again.

Try as I might, there were always a few spare parts left after I thought the clock was together again. And not surprisingly, the shiny bells wouldn't ring! I decided to quietly place the clock back by Mom's bedside, hoping she would never know the difference.

I was rudely awakened the next morning by the frustrated voice of Mother, saying, "Hurry or you'll be late for school. Something's wrong with the alarm clock...it didn't go off!" Looking at me with questioning eyes, she said, "You haven't been messing with the alarm clock, have you?" Knowing that lying would get me in worse trouble than breaking her clock, I grimly replied, "Yes, ma'am." Her response was, "If you can't fix what you broke, you are in big trouble, young man." Knowing I couldn't fix it—I'd already tried!—I pleadingly said, "Big Daddy can fix it!" Her halfhearted reply was, "If Big Daddy can fix it, you're not in trouble!"

"Big Daddy" was the name I affectionately called my grandfather, my mom's father. He was my real-life hero. He could fix anything, do anything, catch anything, cook anything. He had cooked my first fish, and he fixed my broken toys when all hope was lost. I knew Big Daddy could rescue me now! He could fix anything!

That was Wednesday, the night of our regular midweek church service. Big Daddy was the pastor. After church I handed him a crumpled paper bag containing the clock and the extra pieces. With many tears and much weeping, I threw myself on his unfailing wisdom. "I know you can fix it, Big Daddy!" I said, with Mom watching from the foyer.

"I'll take a look at it," he replied while glancing in the paper bag. He told me he'd come over to our house after school the next day. I walked away in confidence mingled with concern. I couldn't help but notice the problematic look that came over his face after he glanced into the bag. *Perhaps this is the one "broken" thing that Big Daddy can't fix,* I thought.

The hours at school passed miserably. As I shuffled home, clinging to hope, I thought, *Big Daddy can do anything.* Shortly after my arrival home, Big Daddy pulled into the driveway. I couldn't help but notice that he was carrying the same crumpled bag I had given him the night before, and I began to entertain the idea of being rescued. He handed me the bag, and I quickly reached inside and took out an alarm clock. It ticked and tocked, and the bells rang! I was saved! Triumphantly, I handed it to my mom. She flashed a knowing look at Big Daddy, who grinned sheepishly. With one last glance, I ran outside to play, with a strange thought dangling...*Wasn't the clock I broke a slightly different color? Oh well, I'm safe...no worries.*

It wasn't until years later that I learned Big Daddy hadn't been able to fix it. So he had shopped all over town to find an almost identical clock to spare his magical reputation and his grandson's posterior! In one sense of the word, he "fixed" the situation, even though he couldn't repair the clock.

There are some times now when I wish my brokenness and broken things could be fixed by "Big Daddy." Life isn't as simple for me now as it was then. But I've carried this lesson with me since that day, and it has often prompted in me a desire to cry out to my heavenly "Big Daddy" to heal my brokenness and repair my life.

I've noticed a lot of "broken" people lately who are overwhelmed by the circumstances of life. You may have been "brokenhearted" yourself over a recent situation, or know someone who has. Psalm 84:5-6 says, "Blessed is the man...who passing through the valley of Baca [which means 'weeping'] make it a well...." We've all passed through valleys of weeping. But I've learned that in the valley of Baca—the valley of weeping—God can turn your weeping into a well of water!

There is a hidden blessing in brokenness!

GodChasers.network newsletter

The Bump in the Road

*D*avid and his crew were trying to handle the holy presence and glory of God with human hands. How do you handle the holiness and glory of God? God will only let you do things your way just so far. I've heard it said that David's caravan "hit a *bump in the road* at the threshing floor." Who put that "bump" in the road? That would be like God! He still has a way of putting speed bumps in the middle of the highway of man's reasoning. They force us to slow down and ask, "Is this the right thing?"

David's problems came when he and his troupe tried to continue on as normal past God's speed bump. The Lord never intended for His glory to creak along on the back of man's mechanisms, vehicles, or programs. He has always ordained for His glory to be transported by sanctified or set apart holy human vessels who reverence and respect His holiness.

Abinadab's sons had spent up to 20 years around the ark. To them, it was an ornate but ordinary box or chest. They were probably honored when they were chosen to drive the cart carrying the ark, but neither one of those young men was prepared, and they didn't know about the ancient warnings concerning God's holiness. When David's procession came to God's holy shaking place in the road, the oxen stumbled and Uzzah reached out to steady the ark. Uzzah's name literally means "strength, boldness, majesty, security" (James Strong, *Strong's Exhaustive Concordance of the Bible* [Peabody, MA: Hendrickson Publishers, n.d.], **Uzzah** [#H5798, #H5797]. Definition adapted from the original definition). The presence of God never needs the assistance or guidance of man's strength to hold its rightful place. Nor will God ever allow the arm of flesh to glory in His presence without tasting death.

God's glory "broke out" on the flesh that drew near to it in a living state and Uzzah was instantly killed. *Only dead men can see God's face*, and only repentant dead flesh can touch His glory.

I don't think any of us have seen the Church function on the order of the church at Jerusalem in the Book of Acts. The deaths of Ananias and Sapphira for lying to God described in Acts 5:1-11 should be reexamined by the Church today. That same Spirit is beginning to visit the Church today, and His standards of holiness have not changed. When the glory of God descended on that young church, it brought fear on the people, but it also brought God's miracle-working power through signs and wonders, causing many to be added to the church (Acts 5:11-16). Why? Because the leaders who were submitted to God flowed in His power and authority. (You have nothing to fear from "Dad" if you haven't done anything bad while "Dad" was gone!)

As soon as God's presence fell on us in small measures of glory, we began asking ourselves the same questions David must have asked himself when he saw how serious it was to be the stewards entrusted with God's manifest presence. We began to ask ourselves, "Should we really be the ones to take care of this sacred Presence?" I distinctly remember saying over and over, "Why me, Lord?" David, the psalmist of the hills and the warrior of God, had suddenly discovered another facet of God's character that he had never seen before. Evidently no one else in Israel had seen this side of God either. Sadly, neither has the Church of today.

David decided to cancel the trip to Jerusalem and pull aside to leave the Presence he now feared at the home of Obededom in nearby Gath (formerly a Philistine stronghold). The ark stayed there for three months, and the Lord blessed Obededom, his family, and everything that he owned.

Why did David stumble like the oxen pulling the cart? He was in shock. He had been doing everything he knew to do in the most respectable manner that he knew of. (In fact, David's methods resemble the methods used by the *Philistines* years earlier to transport the ark into Israelite territory according to First Samuel 6:7.) He was dancing at the head of the procession and around the cart along with the rest of the people while many played instruments and sang. He obviously believed that God would be pleased with his efforts that day.

They were a happy little "church" taking the presence of God to the place where it belonged. Then they hit a holy bump in the road at the threshing floor of *Nachon*, a Hebrew word which ironically means "prepared" (*Strong's*, **Nacon** [#H5225]). They were obviously unprepared. When Uzzah casually reached out to steady "God's box" from falling off of man's vehicle, God seemed to say, "Look, I've let you come this far in your own manner; enough is enough. If you really want My presence back in Jerusalem, then you're going to have to do it My way." Then He struck down Uzzah right on the spot and stopped David's parade in its tracks. *God broke out of His box and caused man's plans to fall* that day, and it would take David three months to recover, repent, research, and return for God's glory. The same thing happens today when we encounter God's manifest glory. Too often we reach out in fleshly presumption to stop the God we've carefully contained in a box from falling off of our rickety man-made ministry program or tradition. We shouldn't be surprised when God's glory breaks out of our doctrinal or traditional boxes and shocks us. Something always dies when God's glory encounters living flesh.

Tommy Tenney – *The God Chasers*

Relinquish What You Don't Understand to Him

It was this power that enabled the men of the New Testament to walk into hostile cities virtually alone. On one such occasion, the Lord told the apostle Paul, "I have many people in this city" (Acts 18:10b NKJV). There wasn't one convert at the time, but God saw something Paul could not see and he had to trust God all the way. The power of relinquishment is the ability to relinquish what we don't understand to a divine mandate. We do not want to walk away from a place in which God sees potential. Where He leads, we must follow, and He will receive all the glory.

Arturo Tuscani was a famous Italian symphony conductor. His specialty was the works of Beethoven. One night in Philadelphia, Pennsylvania, Tuscani conducted the Philadelphia Symphony Orchestra in a program that included the Ninth Symphony, one of the most difficult pieces to direct. It was so majestic and so moving that when the piece was completed, the audience stood for round after round of applause. Tuscani took his bows again and again. He turned to the orchestra; they bowed. The audience continued to clap and cheer. The orchestra members themselves were smiling and clapping. Finally, Tuscani turned his back to the audience, and spoke only to the orchestra. He said, "Ladies, gentlemen—I am nothing. You are nothing. Beethoven is everything."

When you think of this story, remember the divine power of relinquishment. Regardless of how eloquent you are, or how gifted you are with a voice to sing like an angel, *throw yourself at the feet of Jesus and let Him take the serpent out of your gift.*

When men first learned to navigate the open seas using the stars as their "road map," a whole new world opened up to them. Until the development of state-of-the-art satellite positioning technology, the compass was the primary instrument of navigation at sea. It was said, "*He who is a slave to the compass enjoys the freedom of the open sea.*"

Commitment to the compass of God opens the door of the universe to us. When you commit your future to God and let Him set your course, He will direct you to places of unprecedented freedom and usefulness in the Kingdom. First, you must be willing to say with the apostle Paul, "...it is no longer I who live, but Christ lives in me" (Gal. 2:20a NKJV). Declare to Him, "I am nothing. You are everything. Here I am, and here are my gifts, abilities, and dreams, Lord. I throw it all down at Your feet. I give You all, and I hold nothing back."

T.F. Tenney and Tommy Tenney – *Secret Sources of Power*

To Live, You Must Find an Altar and Die

No controversy in the history of man rages hotter than the heated controversy over the blood of Christ. The blood has always offended those with sins to hide and a rebellious will to protect, but few dreamed that it would become a point of offense among so many *in the churches* of America and Europe! The problem is that the blood not only saves the repentant, but it offends and condemns the defiant. It will never be popular among lovers of religion and the popularizers of "divinity through higher human expression and social evolution."

Many churches and respected theologians from the "best seminaries" decided the blood was "out" and the "greasy-grace, easy-sleazy social gospel" was "in" in the late 1800s. The message of "the blood" simply offended the sensibilities of too many civilized congregation members.

The accepted solution was to exchange the uncouth message of the blood for more palatable messages focusing on the more positive aspects of Jesus' teachings. The cross as a symbol of goodness was acceptable for display in church sanctuaries, lecterns, and church signs on the lawn—as long as no one brought up the bloody details of the Lord's passion on Calvary.

No! We should be frightened of a Christ-less, cross-less, bloodless Church. That would be the "perfect church" for satan, but it would do nothing for anyone descended from Adam. Whether it is considered politically correct, socially acceptable, or ministerial suicide, there must be an altar of death and a bloody sacrifice of flesh if we want salvation and power.

Most of us don't want to die, but death is required for those who would live. The bloodied Lamb left no room for debate or self-justification:

> *And he who does not take his cross and follow after Me is not worthy of Me. He who finds his life will lose it, and he who loses his life for My sake will find it* (Matthew 10:38-39 NKJV).

It seems we have become a little afraid of getting too bloody. Church leaders have said among themselves, "If we can handle this 'salvation thing' without blood, if we can make it as painless as possible, we would be so much more popular." Sorry, but there is no way to get around the blood.

Truth, like freedom, is never won conclusively. It must be fought for by succeeding generations. There will be no victory without battle. The way of the cross is a bloody way. We should remember that it was a *gory* way before it became a *glory* way. No, dear friend, if you would live, then you must find an altar and die. A cross awaits you on the other side.

The offense of the blood can be traced to the time after the fall of Adam in the garden of Eden when God Himself shed the first blood to cover the sin of Adam and Eve. He killed an innocent animal to provide a covering or atonement for Adam and Eve. The blood of the innocent for the guilty was required. From that day to this, man has had a built-in theology that without the shedding of blood there is no remission of sin (see Heb. 9:22).

God revealed a new and unspeakable secret about the blood when He engineered the exodus of the children of Israel from Egyptian bondage. He disclosed a new property of the blood of the innocent in the last plague He used to break the will of Pharaoh and punish Egypt for her mistreatment of Joseph's family. This secret is the basis for the Jewish observance of Passover and the foundation of our salvation in Christ.

The plagues that rocked Egypt had failed to shake Pharaoh's stubborn determination to hold the Hebrews in perpetual bondage. That brought Egypt to the final and worst plague of all. The time for the divine exodus was near, and justice would wait no longer. The Lord spoke to Moses and commanded every Israelite household in Goshen (the despised territory of shepherds inhabited by the Israelites), to slay a lamb without blemish and to apply its blood with a bunch of hyssop to the doorposts and lintels of their homes. Their orders were simple: Stay in the house and stay under the blood. (See Exodus 12:1-22.)

T.F. Tenney and Tommy Tenney – *Secret Sources of Power*

Somebody Has to Tend the Fire!

*D*avid did two things to make sure God's presence remained in Jerusalem. First, he prepared a place for God's presence by constructing a tabernacle without walls or a veil. Second, he did something special once the Levites arrived at the tabernacle and set the ark of the covenant in place. He created a "living" mercy seat of worship in the tabernacle so God would be pleased to sit and remain in that humble sanctuary.

David learned a vital secret somewhere in the process of bringing God's presence into Jerusalem. He learned that if you want to keep that blue flame there, *somebody has to tend the fire!* "Do you mean we have to throw logs on the fire?" No, you don't fuel that blue flame of God's *shekinah* presence with earthly fuel. You fuel it through sacrificial worship. *We have no right to call for the fire of God unless we are willing to be the fuel of God.*

David was simply following the heavenly pattern Moses had received for the mercy seat:

> *And you shall make two cherubim of gold; of* **hammered** *work you shall make them at the two ends of the mercy seat. Make one cherub at one end, and the other cherub at the other end; you shall make the cherubim at the two ends of it of one piece with the mercy seat. And the cherubim shall stretch out their wings above, covering the mercy seat with their wings, and they shall face one another; the faces of the cherubim shall be toward the mercy seat* (Exodus 25:18-20 NKJV).

The wings of the cherubim that Moses built touched each other as they encircled and covered the mercy seat where the presence of God would sit just above the lid or "covering." If you read this passage closely, you will notice that the two golden cherubim weren't cast or poured into molds. God said that the gold used to form the covering cherubim had to be "beaten" into the proper shape and position.

The way we can build a mercy seat is to take our positions as purified, "beaten" worshipers. One problem is that God still requires mercy seat worshipers to be formed of gold tried in the fire (purified), conformed (beaten) into the image of perfection, and moved into the proper position of unity for worship. (See Revelation 3:18; Romans 8:29.) This speaks of purity, brokenness, and unity—the three components of true worship under the new covenant of the blood of Jesus. *Brokenness on the earth creates openness in the heavens.*

It is interesting to me that when gold is refined over extreme heat, the first things to come to the top and be skimmed off are the "dross," the obvious impurities and foreign matter. The last thing to be separated from gold is silver, a lesser precious metal that often blends with the raw gold ore. *We often have a hard time separating the "good" from the "best."*

Tommy Tenney – *God's Favorite House*

Victory Begins at a Bloody, Fiery Altar

If this was indeed a brazen altar (whether literal or figurative), then it was an altar where blood fell on coals of fire because it was a bloody altar of sacrifice. Victory begins at a bloody, fiery altar. Even though you see Him high and lifted up, you must also see the blood and fire of the altar of sacrifice.

You may or may not agree with this understanding of Isaiah's vision, but God doesn't waste words. In His divine plan, without the shedding of blood there is no remission (see Heb. 9:22). Isaiah cried out in open confession of sin, fearing for his life because his unredeemed flesh had seen the glory of the Lord. He needed his sins removed and his unworthiness *covered*. He needed the blood somehow, and perhaps the coal from the altar was a bloodstained coal of priceless worth.

This explanation may not be to your satisfaction, but we must agree that it is dangerous for men to get to the fire before they get to the blood. According to the Book of Leviticus, Old Testament priests had to wring out the excess blood of certain animal sacrifices before they dragged the carcass across the altar. Again, we may be at the point of offense, but we have gone too far to turn back. Those priests, though dressed in white, had to bloody that altar from the bottom up and on all sides of the altar before they ever got to the fire. Offensive or not, this speaks loudly to any believer or church earnestly seeking revival today: *There is no shortcut around Calvary to the Upper Room.*

The apostle Paul speaks to each of us with this command: "I beseech you therefore, brethren, by the mercies of God, that you present your bodies a living sacrifice, holy, acceptable to God, which is your reasonable service" (Rom. 12:1 NKJV). There must be a burning of self. The living offering must be placed on an altar of fire and fixed there with no escape. God's message has always been a message of blood first, and then of fire. That is the divine order of progression. You will never make it until you first bloody an altar somewhere. Lay your flesh out before God and make a personal trip to Calvary. Identify yourself with the Lamb of God who died there.

Consider the principle of miracle revealed in the way priests were to certify the cure of lepers among the Israelites. When a leper was finally cleansed, he was to go to the priest and bring with him two birds. The priest would pour water into a basin, kill one of the birds, and allow its blood to mix with the water. Then the priest would bind the living bird to a piece of wood and a sprig of hyssop using a piece of scarlet thread. Finally, the living bird was doused or "baptized" with the blood and water by the "tight hands of the law" represented by the priest.

Immediately the quivering, frightened bird would be taken to an open field where it would be set free-all because of the wood, the hyssop, the scarlet thread, and the blood and water. The bird was *free because of the death of another kind like himself.* He was freed from the clutches of bondage and the law.

T.F. Tenney and Tommy Tenney – *Secret Sources of Power*

The Robes of the Passionate Are Stained With the Marks of Bloody Sacrifice

The triumphant worshipers who entered the gates of Jerusalem carrying the ark of God's glory bore the marks of their struggle to acquire the blue fire of His presence. The ones who labor to restore God's presence and favor are easily distinguished from barren worshipers who stay in the comfort of the city waiting to see what will happen. The robes of the passionate are stained with the marks of bloody sacrifice. The mud and sweat on their priestly robes are visible reminders of their costly journey to bring God's presence from the threshing floor of preparation into their city. (See 2 Samuel 6:6.)

Does that mean that under the new covenant of Christ, we have to jump, hop, and skip to get literally sweaty so God's presence will enter our meetings? No, but we need to be willing to. God, who is Spirit, must be worshiped in spirit and in truth. (See John 4:24.) The self-sacrifice of Jesus Christ on the cross did away with the sacrifice of animals forever, but God never did away with the concept of *sacrifice* in worship.

As we noted earlier, David said that the sacrifices of God are "a broken and contrite heart." You make sacrifices to Him every time you sing hymns and put the virtue of your life into them. As I stated, another way you can "transfer sweat" into the Kingdom is through your giving. When you "sweat" or labor to earn money in the natural realm, you transfer part of yourself to God when you put that freewill offering into the Kingdom. You are transferring value.

Again, I believe that we need to learn what David discovered about the concept of value in sacrifice. Remember, he said, "...I will not sacrifice to the Lord my God burnt offerings *that cost me nothing*" (2 Sam. 24:24 NIV). He knew that the only way to restore God's presence and favor to his people was to sweat the thing out in sacrificial, repentant worship. *If the glory of God is going to come through the gates of the city, somebody has to carry it!*

Everyone who is pursuing revival today will tell you, "This revival stuff is hard work." Ask the ushers, prayer team members, and pastors who have to deal with a press of hungry humanity day after day and week after week in their overcrowded worship facilities. Or ask the intercessors who pray and pry at the cracks in the brass heaven. One man cannot carry the ark of God's glory all the way by himself in this generation. Others have to put their sanctified shoulders under the load on the journey to Jerusalem and say, "Here, let me help."

Tommy Tenney – *God's Favorite House*

Their Captors Watched Them Splatter Blood on Their Doorposts

*U*ntil the plagues came, the Israelites were probably the laughingstock of the Egyptians. As the sun went down on that fateful last night, the Egyptians living nearest to the Israelites may have said among themselves, "What are those crazy Jews doing this time?" as they watched them splattering blood on their doorposts in the fading light. But centuries of spiritual, physical, and mental poverty ended that night. In a matter of hours, prison doors were opened and generations born in bondage were set free.

God used a unique word to describe the importance of the blood of those lambs in Egypt on the first Passover. He said, "The blood shall be a *sign* [or token] for you" (Ex. 12:13a NKJV). A "token" is a small part, a sign, or a symbol of something far greater. If just the merest token of the blood of a lamb accomplished what it did in Egypt before the birth, sacrificial death, and resurrection of Christ, what must the *real thing* be able to accomplish after Calvary? God wants us to find out.

Are we living beneath our privilege? Do we really understand how much the enemy fears the blood of Jesus? How often do we find ourselves at the enemy's mercy because we don't activate the power of the blood and use it by faith? How much do we suffer needlessly because we don't believe in it and exercise faith in its power? There is power in the blood—if we perceive it and apply it in our lives.

Even the lofty vision of Isaiah the prophet seemed to draw its power from an altar of bloody sacrifice. The prophet spoke of a burning coal from an altar that possessed the power to take away iniquity and purge away sin. Upon the death of King Uzziah, Isaiah had been looking at the king's empty throne when he seemed to lift his eyes above the throne to see another higher throne that was never empty. The prophet's vision was transported beyond the earthly into the heavenlies and he declared, "I saw the Lord sitting on a throne, high and lifted up, and the train of His robe filled the temple" (Is. · 6:1b NKJV).

This too is a secret source of power. We must, first of all, personally see the Lord "high and lifted up" above all earthly potentates, heroes, champions, and thrones. As we pin our attention and affection on the exalted Lord, something from Heaven will begin to change our vision and transform our speech.

T.F. Tenney and Tommy Tenney – *Secret Sources of Power*

I Can Almost Smell the Singed Fragrance...

S ometimes I visit places where I can almost smell the singed fragrance of leaves that don't burn. It makes me sense that we're near that place where God is going to give us an encapsulated vision of the greater purpose behind all this.

Most of what we have seen so far is the *renewal* of the Church. I'm thinking that *revival* is not the best word for what we are seeing because it refers to something that is dead being brought back to life. I don't have the terminology to describe what God is about to do. How do you describe a "tsunami"? How do you describe a tidal wave? How do you talk about what God can do, along with the unspeakable grace and strength that come with it?

The biblical model I desire and dream of is God's dealings with the city of Ninevah. I want to see a wave of God sweep through a city, pushing before it all of man's arrogance while leaving behind it nothing but a trail of broken repentance. I'm hungry for revival like we see in Jonah's description of citywide repentance and fasting in Ninevah.

That kind of revival *should have* happened at Nazareth but it didn't. Nazareth would have been the optimal place because that city had the greatest preacher who ever lived. Jesus stood in Nazareth's synagogue and said, "The Spirit of the Lord is upon Me." Then He read from the menu of what He wanted to do—heal the sick, open blind eyes, set the prisoners free—but He wasn't able to do any of it because of the unbelief of the people in Nazareth. We need to pay attention to this sad story because Nazareth was the

"Bible belt" in Jesus' day. Nazareth was the place where it should have happened. (You cannot go by the outward appearance of a place or people.)

I don't care what a thing or a person looks like; only God knows His plans for the future. Many Christians have written off major metropolitan cities such as Los Angeles, New York, Detroit, Chicago, or Houston. Los Angeles may be the home of thousands of pornographic places and the Hollywood film industry, but Ninevah was an even more unlikely place for revival in its day! To say nothing of Shanghai, New Delhi, Calcutta, Rio de Janeiro...and the list grows! But if someone can find the light switch, His glory will flood these cities. It must, because He said that "the glory of God will cover the earth"! (See Numbers 14:21.)

Tommy Tenney – *The God Chasers*

By the Blood, Through the Water, Under the Cloud, Full of the Lamb

God's instruction included the command that the Israelites eat their fill of the sacrificed lamb and unleavened bread in preparation for the exodus. That means the Israelites marched out of Egypt *by the blood*, through the water (of the Red Sea), under the cloud (of God's guiding presence), and full of the lamb that had been slain.

Make no mistake: The message of Exodus chapter 12 is as relevant to us today as it was to the Israelites long ago. If we are to be delivered out of the bondage of sin, we will get out by the shed blood of Jesus, through the water of baptism, under the cloud of God's glory, and full of the Lamb whose body was broken for us. There is power in the blood!

The sacrificed lamb even provided supernatural healing and health for the Israelites. Their deliverance prefigured much of what Christ did on the cross. The Psalmist declared there wasn't a sick person among the crowd of up to three-and-a-half million people! (See Psalm 105:37.)

Just think of a city of that size in America without a single case of back problems, headache, arthritis, cancer, or disability due to deformed limbs or malfunctioning muscles and nervous systems? Do you believe the Book? When the time for the exodus came, every descendant of Abraham walked out from under Egypt's shadow of bondage by the power of the blood of the lamb, and they walked out healed and delivered because they walked out through the door of blood.

Can you imagine what happened when the command came for the Israelites to be ready to leave? Don't you think someone said, "What are we going to do about Grandpa? He's so bent over he can't walk across the room, let alone out of Egypt!" About that time, they heard a loud "Snap! Crackle! Pop!" and then came Grandpa walking straight and ready to go! My friend, there is power in the blood.

T.F. Tenney and Tommy Tenney – *Secret Sources of Power*

Uncontrolled Cravings for Cheap Spiritual Thrills Become "Spiritual Pornography"

We would often rather be vicariously thrilled by God's touch on someone else's life than pursue it on our own. Or, if we are in ministry, we can become addicted to people's infatuation with us because of the anointing. It feels so good to stand in the flow.

Addiction turns even the strongest anointing into a cheap thrill. At its worst, a preacher's uncontrollable craving to minister under the anointing—and a believer's driving compulsion to receive ministry under the anointing—becomes a form of "spiritual pornography." As in the physical variety of this compulsion, "spiritual pornographers" want to get their thrills by observing the intimacy experienced by *others* rather than shouldering the responsibility of *relationship* with God. This is the only proper channel through which we are to derive personal intimacy with God. The Lord doesn't want us to be infatuated with His hands and the blessings they bring to spirit, soul, and body. He wants us to fall head over heels in love with *Him*!

We are essentially saying, "I'm not going to go into God's intimate presence for myself. I'm going to get a cheap thrill out of sharing somebody else's encounter with God. If they are graphic and dynamic, I'll get enough goose bumps to get my anointing fix." When ministers blatantly display the anointing on their life with no regard for pursuing intimacy with God Himself or for leading God's people into personal intimacy with Him, they become "spiritual exhibitionists." They are more concerned with the pleasure derived from their personal display of anointing than with pursuing God's face and ministering to Him. Those who "watch" without pursuing God themselves become mere spiritual "voyeurs" whose lives lack the genuine relationship God desires for them.

We get addicted to the anointing in the same way the children of Israel did. The ministry of Moses and the miracles he did after talking with God clearly represented divine anointing, but God wanted to give the Israelites more. In Exodus 19 He invited everyone in the group to come up and hear Him speak for themselves. This was an opportunity to go *beyond the anointing* and taste of His glory for themselves. The children of Israel said, "Moses, *you* go talk to God and find out what He says. You can have the intimacy—just take some juicy pictures and bring the anointing back to us" (Ex. 20:19, paraphrased). They didn't want to have a God-encounter themselves because it required a relationship that involved responsibility and a death to self.

When you pay the price to encounter God's glory up close and personal, you can't back away from what He tells you because at that point you are "married" to Him. When you get everything secondhand you can say, "It may be or it may not be God. I can't tell because it's just a 'picture of the month.' "

I have tried to send a message to my children by telling one of them to tell the others, "*Dad said.*" *It doesn't work.* If I say, "You go tell your sister that *I said* she needs to clean up her room and rake the yard," the "messenger" of the moment loves to deliver those kinds of messages because they feel empowered, but those messages never have the same impact as the real thing. I can still remember hearing my daughters tell one another after a "second person message" was delivered, "*You're not the boss of me!*" We say that (or the adult equivalent) to our pastors, spiritual leaders, and bosses constantly even though we are adults. All that stops when the heavenly Father shows up personally and manifests His glory.

Tommy Tenney – God's Favorite House

It's Not Going to Be a Cheap Blessing

It is true that all flesh must die in the presence of His glory, but it is also true that all that is of the Spirit *lives forever* in His glory. The eternal part of your being that really wants to live can live forever, but first there is something about your flesh that has to die. Your flesh holds you back from the glory of God, so you are most likely locked in an unending wrestling match between the flesh and the spirit as you read these words. It is time for you to just go ahead and tell Him, "Lord, I want to see Your glory." The God of Moses is willing to reveal Himself to you but it's not going to be a cheap blessing. You will have to lay down and die. He can only come close to you to the degree you are willing to die.

You need to forget who's around you and abandon the "normal protocol." God is in the business of re-defining what we call "church" anyway. He's looking for people who are hot after His heart. He wants a Church of Davids who are *after* His own heart (not just His hand). (See Acts 13:22.) You can seek for His blessing and play with His toys, or you can say, "No, Daddy, I don't just want the blessings; I want You. I want You to come close. I want You to touch my eyes, touch my heart, touch my ears, and change me, Lord. I'm tired of me the way I am, because if I can change, *then the cities can change too.*"

We need to pray for a breakthrough, but we cannot pray for a breakthrough unless we're broken ourselves. Breakthroughs only come to broken people who are not pursuing their own ambition, but who are after the purposes of God. We need to weep over our city just as Jesus wept over Jerusalem. We need a breakthrough from the Lord.

Don't resist the Holy Spirit when the hand of God tries to mold your heart. The Potter of your soul is simply trying to "soften" you. He wants to bring you to such a place of tenderness that it doesn't take a hurricane-force wind from Heaven for you to even know that He is present. He wants you to be so tender that the gentlest breeze from Heaven, the smallest zephyr from His presence, will set your heart a-dancing, and you'll say, "It's Him!"

We need to repent for designing services that men like, instead of yielding to what God likes. Like most men and women, we have wanted "life" in our services when God was after "death" in our gatherings! It is "death" through repentance and brokenness that ushers in the presence of God and causes you to draw near to the Lord and yet *live*.

Some people get very uncomfortable at this point because it's starting to smell a little smoky. They can smell the odor of burning flesh in the air. It may not smell good to us, but God is drawn toward repentance. The Bible says, "When a sinner repents, the angels rejoice" (see Lk. 15:10). Death and repentance on earth bring about joy in the heavenlies.

Revival must begin in your local church before it can reach into your community. If you are hungry for revival, then I have a word from the Lord for you: *Fire doesn't fall on empty altars.* There has to be a sacrifice on the altar for the fire to fall. If you want the fire of God, you must become the fuel of God. Jesus sacrificed Himself to win our salvation, but He has called each and every person who wants to follow Him to do what? To lay down their lives and *take up their cross* and follow Him. (See Luke 9:23.) According to *Strong's Concordance*, the Greek word for "cross," *stauros*, means "figuratively, exposure to death, i.e. self-denial." (James Strong, *Strong's Exhaustive Concordance of the Bible* [Peabody, MA: Hendrickson Publishers, n.d.], **cross** [#G4716].) Elijah didn't ask for God's fire to fall down on the altar until he had loaded it up with fuel and a worthy sacrifice. We've been praying for the fire to fall, but there's nothing on the altar!

Tommy Tenney – *The God Chasers*

Let's Set the Record Straight About the "Great Celestial Conflict"

S ometimes we hear preachers wax poetic with grand descriptions of the "celestial conflict" in Heaven when the archangel lucifer was cast out of God's presence and fell to the earth. It is true that lucifer was cast out of Heaven along with a third of the angels. However, *there was no big fight in Heaven.* (See Isaiah 14:12-15; Luke 10:18.)

The apostle John wrote, "God is light, and in Him is no darkness at all" (1 Jn. 1:5b). God can discern the difference between a thought and an intent (but no one else can). (See Hebrews 4:12.) When something moves from being a thought to becoming an intent, it becomes sin before you ever commit the actual deed. That is why Jesus said that if a man looked on a woman to lust after her, he had crossed the line. (See Matthew 5:28.)

Lucifer was an archangel in charge of the worship in the heavenly realm. The *thought* entered his mind that he would rise up to supersede God, who is the origin of all things. What a silly thought! He should have dismissed it immediately, but he didn't. When the thought of ascending to the throne of God entered lucifer's mind, there was no problem until he said, "I'm going to try that." The moment it moved from a thought to an intent, the tiniest speck of sin appeared in the bright white light of the glory of God—and it was gone in less than a nanosecond. The "war" was declared over and lucifer, now satan, was cast out of there.

Lucifer didn't gather up a third of the angelic corps and say, "Okay, we're going to go to battle for the whole works. We're taking the Big Guy down today." There was no real war. God didn't get up one day and say, "Michael, Gabriel, you guys need to put your swords on. I'm having a problem with lucifer. He is trying to push Me off My throne and I need your help."

There was no cosmic war in Heaven in which God finally managed to prevail and returned to Heaven saying, "Whooo, that was a tough one." It didn't happen like that. The moment lucifer's thought shifted to the realm of intent, in that immeasurable microsecond a tiny speck of darkness appeared in the heavenly realm, He who is Light cast out that darkness instantly. *How long does it take for darkness to flee the room when you flip on the light switch?* There is no battle between photons of light and subatomic particles of darkness. No, when the light comes on, the darkness is obliterated faster than the blink of an eye. That is why Jesus said, "I beheld Satan as lightning fall from heaven" (Lk. 10:18).

In less than a split second, lucifer was stripped of his name, position, and heavenly office, and thrown out of the heavenly glory-filled realm at the speed of light. He barely managed to stay one step ahead of that light as he was cast down, and then darkness fell on the face of the deep.

Satan thought that he had found a place of refuge until God leaned over and saw that the world He had created in absolute beauty had become a place of chaos, void and without form. God corrected that problem by decreeing, "Let there be light." The glory of God fell upon the earth and there was light from the emanation of His own presence—even before He created the sun! (See Genesis 1:3-5,14-19.)

My friend, we face very similar circumstances today: Darkness once again covers the face of the deep. It is interesting to note that the darkness affects only the surface or the "face." *Satan is occupying; he doesn't own.* He is just camping out here because he can't go to the depths of the thing. He's covering all the territory that he can, but his darkness only covers the face of things. His influence is wide, but his strength is shallow!

I remember the time I stood side by side with other believers and looked out over the city of Los Angeles. We prayed and I stretched my hand out toward the valley that is home to about 15 million people. On the face of it, things look pretty dark in that vast city, but it isn't very deep. If you scratch the surface, you will find hungry-hearted people who are just waiting for a flicker of light to come to them. It is that way in your city also! *If worship can ever scratch the surface, the hungry will find you!* They will follow the "light" to its source, just as the wise men of old followed the heavenly light to Christ. Worship opens a window—a window for God's glory to stream down. Humanity is then drawn to the light.

"O God—where is that light switch?! Where is that window?"

It is our job to intercede to the King for the people who dwell in darkness. Like Queen Esther who interceded for the life of her people, we must be willing to pay any price to see God's glory shine upon our churches and cities. *That brings up God's problem.* Sin can't stand in His presence because He is light, and there is no darkness in Him—none at all. Yet He longs to walk with you and me in the cool of the morning as He did with Adam and Eve before they fell into sin.

Tommy Tenney – *God's Favorite House*

Love Not the World So God's Light Will Shine Bright

We have to continually unload our love *of the world* to manifest the Father's love *to the world*. This too is a continuous process because we are continually bombarded by the world's temptations, attractions, and distractions. Love not the world so God's light in your life will shine bright and guide the lost back home. Too often we say we love God, but we prove by our choices that we love ourselves or the world even more. Set your priorities, and let them reflect Him as the first love and top priority in your life.

Don't be surprised if God allows a little crisis situation to challenge you from time to time to help you maintain a healthy level of dependence on Him. After all, He gave the children of Israel fresh manna every day, but made sure it would spoil if kept for more than one day. The point behind this wilderness object lesson was that God did not want His people to ever be more than 24 hours away from proving His promises are true.

Unload your burdens and ensnaring weights upon Him. Share your crisis with the Almighty God for He is able to sustain and preserve you. If you don't learn to unload crisis situations and recurring problems on Him, your mind and heart will grow weary and you will soon stumble.

Finally, keep this fact in mind: Sometimes we have to unload and turn loose of something before God can *give us something better and greater.* The Bible says, "And we know that all things work together for good to those who love God, to those who are the called according to His purpose" (Rom. 8:28 NKJV). The first half of the verse comes easy, but we need to pay equal attention to the second half and remember it is *our* calling, but *His* purpose.

Are you ready and willing to unload? Don't be like some people who have such a tight claim on their problems that they wouldn't take a million dollars for them. Their conversations are peppered with possessive statements like, "*My* heart problem..." and "*My* problems with my children..." Why claim the problems? All that whining only lets the devil know you are in his neighborhood.

Even Jesus had to unload the weight of the cross temporarily. Simon carried the cross of Christ for a distance. If He couldn't reach the destination of His destiny without unloading, neither can you! He unloaded in order to reload and finish the course. Don't let present pressures postpone future destiny. There is power in proper unloading!

The 120 people who gathered together in the Upper Room in Acts chapter 1 had a lot of things to unload, and it seems that Jesus knew that. He specifically said, "Behold, I send the Promise of My Father upon you; but tarry in the city of Jerusalem until you are endued with power from on high" (Lk. 24:49 NKJV). The Greek word translated as *tarry* means to "sit down, settle, and continue" (James Strong, *Strong's Exhaustive Concordance of the Bible* [Peabody, MA: Hendrickson Publishers, n.d.], meanings and definitions drawn from the word derivations for **tarry** [#G2523, #G2516]).

What exactly did those people do in the Upper Room? They waited on the Lord and they *unloaded* every preconceived notion of what they thought God was going to do. They put aside every offense that could separate them and destroy their unity. The seven to ten days the 120 spent unloading in prayer and fasting was followed *by an instantaneous in-filling* of the Holy Spirit! It is time for us to visit the Upper Room again. We need to unload every weight and encumbrance so He can "on-load" His Spirit in power and glory!

T.F. Tenney and Tommy Tenney – *Secret Sources of Power*

It's Not a Pride Thing; It's a Hunger Thing

*T*used to pursue preaching good sermons and great crowds, and attempt great accomplishments for Him. But I've been ruined. Now I'm a God chaser. Nothing else matters anymore. I tell you that as your brother in Christ, I love you. But I love Him more. I couldn't care less about what other people or ministers think about me. I'm going after God. That's not a pride thing; it's a *hunger* thing. When you pursue God with all your heart, soul, and body, He will turn to meet you and you will come out of it *ruined* for the world.

Good things have become the enemy of the best things. I challenge you and release you right now as you read these words to let your heart be broken by the Holy Ghost. It's time for you to make your life holy. Quit watching what you used to watch; quit reading what you used to read if you are reading it more than you read His Word. He must be your first and greatest hunger.

If you are contented and satisfied, then I'll leave you alone and you can safely put down this book at this point and I won't ever bother you again. But if you are hungry, I have a promise from the Lord for you. He said, "Blessed are they which do hunger and thirst after righteousness: for they shall be filled" (Mt. 5:6).

Our problem is that we have never really been hungry. We have allowed things of this realm to satisfy our lives and satiate our hunger. We have come to God week after week, year after year, just to have Him fill in the little empty spaces. I tell you that God is tired of being "second place" to everything else in our lives. He is even tired of being second to the local church program and church life!

Everything good, including the things your local church does—from feeding the poor, to rescuing babies at the pregnancy counseling center, to teaching kids in the Sunday school classes—should flow from the presence of God. Our primary motivating factor should be, "We do it because of Him and because it is His heart." But if we're not careful, we can get so caught up in doing things *for* Him that we forget about *Him.*

You can get so caught up in being "religious" that you never become spiritual. It doesn't matter how much you pray. (Pardon me for saying this, but you can be lost, not even knowing God, and still have a prayer life.) I don't care how much you know about the Bible, or what you know *about* Him. I'm asking you, "Do you *know Him?*"

I'm afraid that we have satiated our hunger for Him by reading old love letters from Him to the churches in the Epistles of the New Testament. These are good, holy, and necessary, but *we never have intimacy with Him.* We have stifled our hunger for His presence by *doing things for* Him.

A husband and wife can do things *for* each other while never really loving each other. They can go through childbirth classes together, have kids, and share a mortgage, but never enjoy the *high level of intimacy* that God ordained and designed for a marriage (and I'm not just talking about sexual things). Too often we live on a lower plane than what God intended for us, so when He unexpectedly shows up in His power, we are shocked. Most of us are simply not prepared to see "His train fill the temple."

The Holy Spirit may already be speaking to you. If you are barely holding back the tears, then let them go. I ask the Lord, right now, to awaken an old, old hunger that you have almost forgotten. Perhaps you used to feel this way in days gone by, but you've allowed other things to fill you up and replace that desire for His presence.

In Jesus' name, I release you from dead religion into spiritual hunger, this very moment. I pray that you get so hungry for God that you don't care about anything else.

I think I see a flickering flame. *He* will "fan" that.

Tommy Tenney – *The God Chasers*

God Will Let You Do Things Your Way (and Let You Pay for It)

When God decided to reveal another facet of His divinity to Abraham and his son Isaac, He did it while taking them through a divine process of preparation we will call "relinquishment." This is the process of releasing, yielding, resigning, surrendering, abandoning, waiving, and giving up something completely.

There is power in relinquishment, but the process isn't much fun at times. It took Isaac up the slopes of Mt. Moriah and left him tied to an altar like a lamb led to slaughter. He wondered if he would live to see the sunset, and he probably wondered why it happened to him. The whole situation was a result of something he had nothing to do with! Isaac didn't know in advance what role he would play in God's purposes, so *all he could do was relinquish himself to the process.*

Abraham didn't understand what was going on either. God's request that he sacrifice Isaac was totally out of character with the God he had known in the past. All Abraham could do was relinquish his son and trust God. By faith, he must have said, "Lord, if I kill Isaac, I know You are able to raise him from the dead. Your word is true and You promised me You would make a mighty nation out of him." Can you imagine the load Abraham carried up that mountain?

Moses could speak to us about relinquishment too. He knew God had called him to deliver the children of Israel, but he wanted to do it his own way. He was wearing the clothing of a prince of Egypt when he went sauntering forth and saw an opportunity. He saw an Egyptian beating a Hebrew slave and this deliverer decided it was time to rise to the occasion and take things into his own hands. At the end of the story a man was dead. That is the Egyptian way.

Moses was about to learn that God will not use an unwilling servant. If you want something badly enough that God has withheld from you, then God will let you have it. He will not fight you for the relinquishment of your will. If you want to take things in your own hands and do things your own way, God will allow you to do so. He will step back and say, "Okay, go ahead." The Israelites found out the hard way:

> *They soon forgot His works; they did not wait for His counsel, but lusted exceedingly in the wilderness, and tested God in the desert. And* **He gave them their request, but sent leanness into their soul** *(Psalm 106:13-15 NKJV).*

Moses' "Egyptian way" is never what God has in mind. The Bible tells us that Moses "looked this way and that way" before he murdered the Egyptian (Ex. 2:12 NKJV). *What he failed to do was look up!* He wanted to know if men were looking and evidently he wasn't concerned by the fact that God was watching. God said, "Okay, Moses. The first thing I have to teach you is where you get your orders. You won't be so interested in audience response then. It matters little if anyone is watching."

Moses probably thought he had done a good deed. After all, he had saved an Israelite. Perhaps he even told himself, "One down; ten million to go." Then Moses dug a little hole and *buried his mistake in the sand.*

Not too many days passed before God openly exposed the works of Moses' flesh and made it known. Once he stepped out of the will of God, Moses couldn't even keep one Egyptian buried in the sand. *When he stepped back into the will of God, however, he was able to bury the entire army of Pharaoh in the bed of the Red Sea!* Moses tackled a job doing it one at a time, but he didn't do it in God's time or God's way. God had a better plan, a better time, and a better way.

T.F. Tenney and Tommy Tenney – *Secret Sources of Power*

Daddy, We're Tired of Playing Man-made Games

*H*is answer is, "Yes," but it is only because He will do anything to commune with us. He will even put "His strength into captivity" (Ps. 78:61) to come sit with us because He is so desperate for us to be with Him. But He is really waiting for us to say, "Daddy, we're tired of playing the man-made games of church. Will You take us to the big house for real communion?"

I'm tired of coming home from church with nothing changed. I'd rather come back from an encounter with God limping instead of leaping—just so my destiny is different.

You may not like the feeling of frustration, but you need to understand that *some frustrations are holy frustrations*. Just like *some hunger is holy hunger*, it is planted by God to produce something. I didn't say it; He said it: "Blessed are those who hunger and thirst" (Mt. 5:6a NKJV).

Holy hunger and blessed frustrations can produce a destiny-altering wrestling match. You should try to lose this fight...but not until you are scarred by God's touch. God's touch permanently shriveled Jacob's tendon—so much so that Jews wouldn't eat "Jacob" tendon from any animal. Hebrew dietary codes forbid eating things that have died. God put a handle of "death" in Jacob's life in order to secure his future. *Flesh-death often produces future destiny. Your program may die for His purpose to live.*

I think that we are so full with careers and agendas and man-made machinery that we have lost the simplicity of the manifested presence of God. We desperately need to take up John the Baptist's motto and put it to work in our lives: "*He must increase, but I must decrease*" (Jn. 3:30). It is time to call out the Jacobs who have grown so sick of themselves that they will wrestle with their destiny until they've been touched by God—*even if they come home with a permanent limp and an eternal change of heart.*

> *Change my heart, O God!*
> *Change my path, I pray!*
> *Touch me with Your rod...*
> *So I will go Your way.*

Tommy Tenney – *God's Favorite House*

You Can't Seek His Face and Save Your "Face"

When God tells us, "You can't see My face," most of us are satisfied that we've done our religious duty and we quickly return to life as usual. When we discover that God's best and deepest treasures require death to self, we often don't pursue Him any further. We don't ask the questions we need to ask to find out *why* His presence doesn't come cheaply. Perhaps it's because we think it is impertinent or we are simply afraid of His answer. Moses persisted. He had learned that *it isn't impertinent to pursue God for His own sake; it is God's greatest desire and delight.*

This burning desire to see God's glory, to see Him face to face, is one of the most important keys to revival, reformation, and the fulfillment of God's purposes on the earth. We need to look closely at the 1,500-year pursuit of God's glory by the ancient patriarch, Moses. As we noted earlier, when Moses told God, "Show me Your glory," the Lord said, "You can't, Moses. Only dead men can see My face." Fortunately Moses didn't stop there. Unfortunately, the Church did.

It would have been easy for this man to have been satisfied with God's first answer, but he wasn't. Moses wasn't selfish or presumptuous. He wasn't seeking material things or personal fame. He wasn't even seeking miracles or gifts (and Paul even instructed us to seek after the best gifts in his letter to the Corinthians). Moses simply wanted *God*, and that is the greatest gift and blessing we can ever give Him. Yet Moses had to *pursue* Him, and it didn't come easy.

*And [Moses] said, I beseech Thee, **show me Thy glory**.*

And He said, I will make all My goodness pass before thee, and I will proclaim the name of the Lord before thee; and will be gracious to whom I will be gracious, and will show mercy on whom I will show mercy.

*And He said, **Thou canst not see My face: for there shall no man see Me, and live**.*

And the Lord said, Behold, there is a place by Me, and thou shalt stand upon a rock:

And it shall come to pass, while My glory passeth by, that I will put thee in a clift of the rock, and will cover thee with My hand while I pass by:

*And I will take away Mine hand, and **thou shalt see My back parts: but My face shall not be seen*** (Exodus 33:18-23).

By the time Moses had this discussion with God, the Israelites had already turned their backs to run from God when He asked them to draw near on Mount Sinai. It was Moses who had boldly pressed into the cloud of His presence. In fear and trembling, Israel demanded that Moses and the Aaronic priesthood stand between them and the God they feared because of their sin. Moses often walked into the concealing cloud in the tent of meeting, and somehow he dared to desire even *more*.

Tommy Tenney – *The God Chasers*

Have We Picked Up "Egyptian Shadows"?

Isaiah the prophet spoke of those who "trust in the shadow of Egypt." (See Isaiah 30:2-3.) Some trust in "Egypt" for protection from their enemies, but far more are simply influenced when they get in its shadow. The biblical "shadow of Egypt" shades them from full light. We can pick up "Egyptian shadows" in the biblical sense, though not living as an Egyptian. That was what Moses was doing. This "shadow-proofing" is an unavoidable part of the relinquishment training plan for everyone who is called to exercise leadership at any level in God's Kingdom.

When Moses threw down his favorite old shepherd's rod, it became a serpent and he literally ran from it. (See Exodus 4:3-4.) Things got worse when God said, "Pick it up by the tail." Nearly everyone knows that is a foolish thing to do because that leaves the "business end" of the snake loose and free for action.

It didn't make much sense to throw down the rod, but it made no sense at all to pick up the snake by the tail! Moses had been in the desert a long time and he knew a poisonous adder when he saw one. But God told him to pick it up by the tail.

During your training trip through the wilderness of relinquishment, you will probably think God is leading you the wrong way, or that He is saying something that doesn't make sense. God's commands aren't always accompanied by explanations. The point is that even when we cannot figure out what God is doing, we must trust Him.

When Moses reluctantly picked up the snake it became a rod again. From this place forward in the narrative, that rod is never again referred to as "the rod of Moses." It is referred to as "the rod of God." (See Exodus 4:1-20; 17:9.) Because Moses released it and the snake was taken out of it, it was God's rod. The one thing Moses thought he could trust in the most had to be relinquished to God. God may strip you of everything in order to let you see and understand your total dependence on Him. With that stripping, with that relinquishment, comes power. Sometimes there are things we just want to hold onto that we have to release so God can remove the snake from it.

Our nation is rapidly being conformed to the image of the world, with its many gods and "many paths to salvation." Americans are worshiping demonic power, the occult, pleasure, and even death itself. For more than a decade, many of the top television shows and movies have prominently featured witchcraft, the occult, and the demonic. However, the greatest idol of all on the American scene is the worship of man and of self.

God is looking for something or *someone* to silence these false prophets of the profane. *We need something that will shut the mouths of the gainsayers today,* and it won't happen with better debaters, louder preachers, superior training programs, or larger sound systems. None of these things are bad or evil, but *the only thing that will do it right is the power of God expressed through a selfless life.*

T.F. Tenney and Tommy Tenney – *Secret Sources of Power*

You Must Dismantle Your Glory to Minister to Him

God spoke to me and said, "Mary dismantled her glory to minister to Me." If all the disciples were present, there were at least 12 other people in that room that day, and not one of them attained the intimacy that she obtained that day. The disciples missed it, even though they were good people like Peter, James, and John. Hear me, friend; you can be busy being a disciple and *doing the work*, but *miss the worship*! Do you really think God needs us to *do things* for Him? Isn't He the Creator who stepped out on the balcony of Heaven and scooped out the seven seas with the palms of His hands? Wasn't it God who pinched the earth to make the mountains? Then obviously He doesn't need you to "do" anything. What He wants is your *worship*. Jesus told the woman at the well, "...true worshippers shall worship the Father in spirit and in truth: for *the Father seeketh such to worship Him*" (Jn. 4:23).

Like countless numbers of pastors, elders, and deacons in the Church today, the disciples got nervous when faced with such raw hunger for God and were saying, "Somebody stop this woman!" But Jesus intervened and said, "No, finally *somebody is doing something that's right*. Don't you dare stop her!" The Church doesn't make room for Marys with alabaster boxes because they make all the rest of us nervous when they begin to dismantle their glory, pride, and ego right there "in front of everybody." (The real problem is that our ego and self-centered glory stands out like a flashing beacon in the place of humility.)

God is saying to His people, "I will bring you close to Me *if you will dismantle your glory.*" I keep hearing Him say, "Dismantle your glory; take your ego apart and lay it aside. I don't care who you are, what you feel, or how important you think you are. I want *you*, but first you must dismantle your glory." Why? Because the burial of man's glory is often the birth of God's glory.

Mary had to get to the point where her passion made her say, "I don't care who sees me do this." You may feel a tugging and drawing in your heart as you read these words. If that is true, then I can almost guarantee that you have learned how to keep a straight face and "keep going" even though you felt like falling at the Lord's feet to ask for mercy and forgiveness. You must let your love break past the shell of "who you pretend you really are." God wants you to openly and boldly let the world know how much you really love Him—even if you have to dismantle your glory right in front of a room full of disdaining disciples. Become a box-breaker! Break the box of "your" precious things and finalize it by a public show of private passion.

God doesn't need your religious service; He wants your worship. And the only worship He can accept is worship that comes from humility. So if you want to see Him, you will have to dismantle your glory and bathe His feet in your tears—no matter what you may find there. (Honestly, isn't that about the only thing your glory is good for? Our righteousness is as a filthy rag in His sight.8)

Tommy Tenney – *The God Chasers*

God Is Committed to Character, Not Talent

What is in your hand? Ability? A fine mind? Power to influence people? Eloquence? Personality? Talent? Throw it down—there might be a snake in it! Regardless of our personal talents and abilities, God is committed to character, not talent. He wants us to be totally dependent on Him. What is in your hand? Let God have it. There could be a little sin left in it. A little serpent life might be there that you don't even know about.

We must take our gifts—whatever they may be—and cast them at the feet of Jesus. Let Him take the serpent—the flesh—out of them and give them back to us. Then they become the power of God in our lives. Where leadership is concerned, that even includes the "approval" of the people you lead. Leadership can be lonely at times, and misunderstanding seems to be part of the leadership package. Even Jesus had to live with misunderstanding throughout His earthly ministry, and after all, He was *perfect*. The rest of us should expect to run into some problems that call for even more relinquishment along the way.

Moses didn't fit the stereotype of a great leader. His first attempt to help his people led to murder, rejection by the Hebrews, and a frantic flight into the wilderness. To say he was totally misunderstood might be an understatement. The misunderstanding became stronger the longer the Israelites marched through the wilderness.

Finally, a Levite leader named Korah rose up with 250 top Israelite leaders and publicly challenged Moses' leadership. Moses fell to the ground and humbly buried his face in the sand, and God showed up in righteous anger and instantly buried Korah and his cohorts in the sand. Those men didn't understand that Moses' power came from his humble relinquishment of *everything* to the Lord. (See Numbers 16.) Moses also knew what it was like to have his own family misunderstand him. Miriam and Aaron, his older sister and brother, even tried to usurp his authority one time, but once again God stepped in and settled the matter. (See Numbers 12.) Sometimes those closest to you— your own family—will be the ones who misunderstand.

Why did Jesse bring all his sons *except David* when the prophet invited him to a sacrifice *with his sons?* (See 1 Samuel 16:11.) David wrote, "Behold, I was brought forth in iniquity, and in sin my mother conceived me" (Ps. 51:5 NKJV). It is interesting that this is the only mention of David's mother in the Bible, other than when he asked the King of Moab for asylum for his "father and mother" (1 Sam. 22:3 NKJV).

Have you ever wondered if David was an illegitimate child? Perhaps his father did not consider him to be one of his true sons. It is just a thought, but if it is true, then it only reinforces the power of relinquishment. This is the power that helped David leave his history in his past! God has been known to take the downcast and illegitimate and make them legitimate!

God saw past the surface and peered into David's heart. When young David told King Saul he would go out to meet Goliath in battle, he didn't brag, "Watch how good my aim is!" He didn't even mention the slingshot and the five smooth stones or the fact that he had just enough "ammunition" for Goliath. He just said, "The Lord, who delivered me from the paw of the lion and the paw of the bear, He will deliver me from the hand of this Philistine" (1 Sam. 17:37a).

T.F. Tenney and Tommy Tenney – *Secret Sources of Power*

I'm a Walking Dead Man

O nly dead men see God's face, so when you go behind that veil you have to say, "I'm really not alive anymore. I'm a walking dead man." When a condemned man begins his final walk to the death chamber, just before they close the door of the corridor, the warden or one of the chief guards will often shout through the hall, "*Dead man walking.*" This is to let everyone know that a man is spending his last few moments of life on this earth, and that they are to be still and honorable. The man is alive, but only for a few moments. When he gets to the death chamber, it's all over. That is how a Christian lives out Romans 12:1: *dead man walking.*

The high priest of old knew that he was a "dead man walking" when the other priests tied a rope around his ankle while he looked at the heavy veil separating him from the Holy of Holies. The only way he would ever walk out of that room alive was solely by the mercy and grace of God. We don't understand the delicate matter of approaching the glory of God today. We talk about the glory and say, "The glory is here," but it really isn't. The *anointing* is here, and there may be a measure of the light of God. But if the glory of God ever showed up in full measure, we'd all be dead. Mountains melt at His manifest presence; how much more man's flesh! (See Judges 5:5; Nahum 1:5.)

We have failed to grasp something about the glory of God (perhaps we are unable to grasp it). Paul the apostle said, "That no flesh should glory in His presence" (1 Cor. 1:29). If there is flesh present when the glory of God comes, then it will have to be *dead* flesh, because nothing can live in that presence. The only mortal thing that can remain in His manifest presence and stand is "dead" flesh, because only dead men can see His face.

Once a year the high priest of Israel would leave his home with a heavy heart and tell his family, "I don't know if I'm coming back. I'm not sure, but I think I've done everything I'm supposed to do. Is my ephod on straight?" The Jews were so cautious about avoiding defilement that the high priest was not even allowed to sleep the night before he went behind the veil! The other priests kept him up all night reading the law to him, so that he wouldn't accidentally defile himself through a dream in the night.

Allegorically speaking, when the moment of truth finally came, the high priest would carefully dip his finger into the warm blood of the sacrificial goat or lamb and daub it on his earlobes. He would apply more blood to each of his thumbs and on his big toes. Why? Symbolically, he was taking on the appearance of one who is *dead* so he could come near God's glory and yet live. Once the blood of death was applied head and toe, the priest would take a deep breath and take one last look at the mortal realm, double-check the rope around his ankle, and reach for the censer. This bowl or container connected to a chain had hot embers in the bottom. The priest would take a handful of holy incense and drop it on top of the embers, which would create a thick billowing cloud of sweet-smelling smoke. The priest would stick this censer under the veil and swing it back and forth until smoke completely filled the Holy of Holies. Then he would gently lift the bottom hem of the heavy veil and crawl into the Most Holy Place with fear and trembling, desperately hoping he would come back alive. *Knees are better than feet for entering the Holy of Holies.*

Tommy Tenney – *The God Chasers*

Don't Rob Yourself of Forgiveness by Clinging to Unforgiveness

*H*ere is a vital scriptural principle: *You are only forgiven as you forgive others.* (See Matthew 6:14.) If you cling to unforgiveness toward another person, you are robbing yourself of your own forgiveness from God. Forgiveness toward others doesn't come naturally, it comes supernaturally.

Have you ever had to "work on" having a bad spirit? If you are like every other human being on earth, it just comes naturally to your flesh. We never have to work on being resentful. Have you ever had to tell yourself, "You know, he did me wrong and I'm going to have to work up a good case of resentment against him; it may take me three or four days to get it going good, but I'm going to work up a good case of resentment and get myself a bad spirit"? No, it just doesn't happen that way.

When resentment rises up, it comes without our even thinking about it; it is virtually instant. Forgiveness, on the other hand, takes a conscious choice and effort on our part. Our job, as born-again Christians, is to work on keeping a good attitude, a sweet spirit, and a pure heart before God and other people. This is impossible unless we learn the power of forgiveness and make right choices along the way.

Many Christians deal with another problem that is described in the statement, "I just can't forgive myself for that." This is a preposterous statement once we realize what is really being said: "Jesus, what You did on Calvary is not good enough for me." Once you have confessed your sin and found Christ in the power of the Holy Spirit, you are transformed into a new creature and the "guilty you" dies. From that moment on, if you cannot forgive yourself, it is an insult to Calvary.

If *God* forgives you, who do you think you are to say you can't forgive yourself? Are you higher and mightier than God? Are you smarter than He is? That is what your words and actions imply. The Bible says, "Therefore if the Son makes you free, you shall be free indeed" (Jn. 8:36 NKJV). Accept His forgiveness! Forgive yourself! If the enemy throws something back in your face, just say, "I thank God you keep reminding me of that, devil. *I've been forgiven!* Praise God!"

T.F. Tenney and Tommy Tenney – *Secret Sources of Power*

You Could Never Repay Me, but You Are Forgiven

There is power in forgiveness. Do you remember Jesus' parable about the man who owed his king ten thousand talents? (See Matthew 18:23-35.) Scholars place widely varying values on this amount, but all of them agree it was an impossibly high amount for any employee to ever pay back. If we take a middle-of-the-road estimate, then this servant owed his king ten million dollars. His monthly income plus "bonuses" probably couldn't have even paid the monthly interest on such a sum.

When the king ordered that the man and his family members be sold to recover the debt, the man begged him, *"Forgive me! I'll repay you someday."* The king said, *"No. You'll never be able to repay me. I'll forgive the whole debt. You are forgiven."* Can you imagine how happy that man must have been? His ten-million-dollar debt had been *forgiven* and marked "Paid in Full"!

This happy man had also been owed some money, so he decided to seek out a fellow servant who owed him "a hundred pence" or only 20 dollars. Evidently, he had "loaned" the second man money from the same fortune he borrowed from the king. After being forgiven for a ten-million-dollar debt, surely this man went to tell the good news to his debtor and forgive his tiny debt as well...or did he? The Bible says, "He laid hands on him and took him by the throat, saying, 'Pay me what you owe!' " (Mt. 18:28b NKJV)

This man who had been forgiven for a multi-million-dollar debt showed no mercy to the man who owed him only 20 dollars; instead he had him thrown into jail until he could repay his debt. Our sins always find us out. The man's fellow servants were so angry when they saw what he did that they told the king. The king canceled the man's pardon and placed him in the hands of tormentors or torturers until he repaid his debt. Jesus bluntly warned His listeners then and now: "So My heavenly Father also will do to you if each of you, from his heart, does not forgive his brother his trespasses" (Mt. 18:35 NKJV).

If you have that kind of spirit, cancel it. The only money the unmerciful servant had available to loan to his victim was the money loaned to him by the king! He should have offered his debtor some of the forgiveness he had received from the king. The only forgiveness we have to give is what we receive from God. We aren't any different from the servant who owed an unpayable debt: The Lord has forgiven each of us of a "multi-million-dollar debt." Don't you think we should be quick to forgive our brother or sister of their "20-dollar debt" to us? (We can't afford to say, "No.")

T.F. Tenney and Tommy Tenney – *Secret Sources of Power*

Many Have Become "Milk Babies" in Padded Pews

*U*nfortunately, the Israelites suffered from the same problem many Christians do today. We have become addicted to the anointing, the relayed word of good preaching and teaching. Too many of us have become "milk babies" who want to sit on padded pews in an air-conditioned and climate-controlled building where someone else will pre-digest what God has to say and then regurgitate it back to us in a half-digested form. (We're afraid of getting "spiritual indigestion" from messages we think are "too rough" to handle.) *Tender tummies are unused to tough truth!*

The solution is hunger and desperation for God Himself without intermediaries. We need to pray, "God, I'm tired of everybody else hearing from You! Where is the lock on my prayer closet? I'm going to lock myself away until I hear from You for myself!"

We make a great deal out of reading the Word and that is important. But we need to remember that the early Church didn't have access to what we call the New Testament for many years. They didn't even have the Old Testament Scriptures because those expensive scrolls were locked up in synagogues. The only Scriptures they had were the verses from the law, the Psalms, and the prophets that had been passed down orally from grandfathers and grandmothers—and that only if they were Jewish believers. So what *did* they have? They walked and talked with *Him* in such a rich level of intimacy that it wasn't necessary for them to pour over dusty love letters that were written long ago. They had God's love notes freshly written on their hearts.

The Holy Spirit is saying, "Look, I know it's great that I've brought you out of sin and your clothes aren't wearing out. You are living in a measure of blessing, and you have My presence revealed in the cloud and the fire every day. I know you've got good leadership, but what *I* really want is this: I want to grow you up and I want to pull you close in a new level of intimacy."

No true revival has ever occurred simply because people sought revival. They were birthed when people *sought Him.* In our presumptuous thinking, we have said, "Okay, we're going to hold a revival." You might as well try to hold a hurricane! If you can hold it, then "it ain't revival." If you can contain it or control it, then "it ain't revival either." We need to call it what it is: a series of good meetings complete with whipped-cream preaching and maraschino cherries of man on top! We may love it and lick our lips through every minute of it, *but it isn't revival.* We have to face the fact that we have become addicted to all the things that accompany church, like the choirs and the music. But they are not what God calls "church" and they are not true revival either. I have a strong sense that God is about to strip all that away to ask us, "Now, who loves *Me*? Who wants *Me*?" It's time to seek the Reviver instead of revival!

God is tired of having *long distance relationships* with His people. He was tired of it thousands of years ago in Moses' day, and He is tired of it today. He really wants to have intimate, close encounters with you and me. He wants to invade our homes with His abiding presence in a way that will make every visitor begin to weep with wonder and worship the moment they enter.

Tommy Tenney – *The God Chasers*

Forgiveness Exploded Two Directions on the Human Timeline

Thank God that Jesus was not merely speaking to the profane and the perplexed who gathered around the cross two thousand years ago. Those few words from the Savior's mouth exploded in "both directions" on the timeline of human existence.

The forgiveness offered by God's Son carried the potential to forgive and cover the sins of every human being who lived in the ages prior to His brutal death on the cross at Calvary. It also carried forward in time from the bloody Mount outside Jerusalem to forgive and cover all the sins of man until His victorious second coming as Lord of lords and King of kings. The only catch to the miracle is that each person must admit their *need* for forgiveness, and choose to *receive* it from Christ Jesus as their Lord and Savior.

The power of forgiveness cannot be forced upon the unwilling, nor can it be forced by human effort or diligence to flower in barren human hearts. True forgiveness is a product of Heaven alone. It unfolds in human experience through our impossibly diverse climates like the petals of a flower. To learn its lesson, we must find the perfect bloom at the cross of Calvary. It is the summit of the world's highest hopes and the abyss of the world's deepest sorrow.

The cross marks the place where God, robed in a regalia of battered but sinless human flesh and the bloodied garments of the condemned, courted and won our love with His life's blood. It is the place where divine power withheld its might while grace worked its greatest miracle. The sweetest story of God is the story of our Lord's victory on Calvary's bitter cross. It is God's "Ph.D. dissertation" and magnum opus on the immeasurable power of forgiveness.

When Jesus said, *"Forgive...,"* the hordes of hell were bound, and satan felt the first chill signaling his miserable defeat. Within three hours, the suffering was complete and the Lord Jesus announced to the Father that His job was done. (See Luke 23:44-47.) Unseen hands grasped the heavy woven veil separating worshipers from the Holy of Holies in the temple and ripped it down the middle from the top to the bottom—a feat impossible for any mortal man.

Mercy danced out from the heavenly mercy seat, passed through the empty Holy of Holies and the rent veil of Herod's temple to skip and twirl down the streets of Jerusalem and touch a repentant thief on one side of Jesus. Then she reached down to transform the heart of the centurion directing the Roman soldiers at the foot of the cross. She continued her dance of joy to Jerusalem's silent graveyards to kick open several tombs so certain departed saints could enjoy an early resurrection and revisit their shocked loved ones in the city. (See Matthew 27:52-54.)

Finally, Mercy dove into hell and wrestled the keys from the devil himself and came out triumphantly shouting, "I am He who lives, and was dead, and behold, I am alive forevermore" (Rev. 1:18a NKJV). Then Jesus led captivity captive and brought forth the keys to death, hell, and the grave. (See Ephesians 4:8.) Can we comprehend what *power* was released in the universe when Jesus said, "Forgive"?

We must all come into the presence of forgiveness, but why should we examine such basic truths? Because it is possible—and probable—that many of the people in church congregations around the world enjoy the "culture" of church without being *changed* by an experience with God. Nothing we can say or write can typify or describe the transforming, cleansing power of God; the only way to experience it is by receiving God's forgiveness and then giving it to others. It is there, in God's forgiveness, that we find the power of a new life, the power of new hope, and the power of new joy.

T.F. Tenney and Tommy Tenney – *Secret Sources of Power*

Jesus Affected Three Worlds When He Said, "Forgive"

hen Jesus prayed, "Father, forgive them," His words reached back in time to enfold the entire history of man before the Lord's incarnation. They covered the "present world" of His day, and reached ahead to the world that would exist after His return to Heaven. Now two thousand years or more after Jesus uttered those words, we are covered with divine forgiveness and pardon.

The day God forgave, flesh was affected, angels were affected, hell was affected, demons were affected, and the devil himself was bound. No matter how bad your life has been, the river of God's forgiveness will flow again into the cold, bitter, and hardened valleys of your heart when you come into the presence of forgiveness.

When forgiveness is present, the enemy of your soul has to back up without a word being said to him. His hands are tied and he cannot work in the presence of forgiveness. *Forgiveness puts the handcuffs of Heaven on hell itself.*

Have you ever heard someone ask, "How can I forgive someone who doesn't ask for that forgiveness?" The answer should be: "Ask Jesus." Show me one man or woman kneeling at the cross of Calvary and looking up into the face of the dying Savior to say, "Forgive us." According to the Bible's scores of eyewitnesses, no one was asking Jesus for forgiveness that day. It just didn't happen. He said, "Forgive them..." *anyway.*

No one asked for it. No one negotiated for it. The battle-hardened Roman soldiers driving the nails, and the hard-hearted religious hypocrites who put the Lord into their hands for execution, could have cared less at the moment whether He forgave them or not. The word *forgiveness* didn't come up in the usual chatter at crucifixion time.

The cross should always remind us that forgiveness is not cheap. What Jesus gives you is not a gimmick to give you goose bumps. It is not the product of a pep rally, or some seminar-induced positive mental attitude that you can prime like some moral pump. The kind of forgiveness Jesus brings to our lives triggers radical reconstruction of the human heart! When forgiveness is released, there is incredible power. The hand of God shattered the boundaries in every known dimension through the power of release *when Jesus forgave.*

Every one of us must deal with certain circumstances in life that cannot be changed. Perhaps Peter the fisherman wished that he could have borrowed the classic education Paul received at the feet of the renowned Jewish teacher, Gamaliel, but he would always remain Peter from Galilee. For centuries, Christians have remembered Peter as the "man who was unlearned," but who astounded the teachers of the Law who "took note that he had been with Jesus." (See Acts 4:13.)

Jesus transformed the life of Mary Magdalene the prostitute, but she still probably wished that she could undo the mistakes and pain of her past. She couldn't. Mary faced the same choice we all face: She could remain a slave to unforgiveness by clinging to her anger and resentment toward the men who abused her and the people who rejected her; or she could accept God's forgiveness, choose to forgive, and begin a life of freedom. We know the choice Mary made. What about you?

T.F. Tenney and Tommy Tenney – *Secret Sources of Power*

All They Want to Do Is "Date" God

There is something in us that makes us afraid of the commitment that comes with real intimacy with God. For one thing, intimacy with God requires *purity*. The days of fun and games in the Church are over. What do I mean by "fun and games"? If your definition of fun is "low commitment and lots of thrills and chills," then all you've ever wanted to do is "date God." You just wanted to get in the backseat with Him. Do I need to draw a picture? God is tired of us wanting to get our thrills from Him without putting on the ring of commitment! Some are more enamored with the "goose bumps" than the glory! They're addicted to the anointing, liking the feeling of being blessed, receiving the "gifts" like a religious "gold-digger," happy with chocolates, flowers, and jewelry. The last time I checked, He was still looking for a bride, not a girlfriend; one who will "stick" with Him.

I'm afraid that many people in the Church have simply approached God to get what they can from Him without committing anything in return. God is saying to His Church, "I don't want that. Now if you want to marry Me, let's do this right. Let's pledge ourselves to each other." We've chased after cheap thrills without the commitment, but God is saying, "Intimacy." And He's saying it everywhere: "Intimacy." And *out of that intimacy* will come revival. The babe of revival is hewn from the granite rock of commitment to the Bridegroom. Babies are always birthed from intimacy. It's time to "draw near."

We've often placed the cart before the horse. We say, "We want revival," and never mention intimacy. We seek revival without seeking

Him. That's a lot like some stranger of the opposite sex walking up to you and saying, "I want kids. What do you say? I don't really know you and I'm not even sure I like you. Of course, I don't want all the commitment that goes with marriage, but I really do want children. How about it?"

Leaders in the Church have written countless books on how to grow churches, but sometimes the underlying message there is, "This is how to grow churches without relationship with Him." We have tried to find shortcuts to short-circuit the "intimacy requirement" every way we can. Why? It is because what we want is a "bunch of kids" sitting on the pews in the church so we can look around and compare with everybody else's church family in town. Children in and of themselves do not make a household! They are the natural by-product of a loving relationship and intimacy in a marriage. Frankly, most of our churches today are the spiritual equivalent of a dys-functional household—"single parent" presbyteries. Where is "Dad"?

What we really need to be seeking is a *real relationship with God.* Anytime you put a man and a woman together who love each other, you don't have to worry about whether or not they will have children in most cases. It's a natural outgrowth of the process of intimacy.

Why is it that the largest revivals in the last century have never been held on American soil? I think it dates to the era when our morals went down the tubes along with our commitment levels. I pro-pose that our nation's collective ability to really grow deep in its rela-tionship with God is accurately mirrored in its reciprocal (or opposite) factor—by our skyrocketing trend toward rampant divorce rates and broken marriages. In other words, we have forgotten or dismissed as unimportant the lost art of commitment to God. As we made the choice to turn away from God's face at the mountain, every other commitment in our lives began to deteriorate and fall apart as well.

Tommy Tenney – *Extreme GodChasers*

The Persecuted Must Live in a Constant Spirit of Forgiveness

Christians living under constant persecution could not survive if they did not get up every morning and say, "I forgive this system. I forgive these soldiers. I forgive this government. I forgive these circumstances." They will tell you that a tremendous power surge of the Holy Spirit accompanies a spirit of forgiveness. It gives them grace to stand and win in spite of seemingly impossible circumstances.

When Jesus Christ comes into our lives, He brings divine forgiveness with Him. He equips us with the power of forgiveness, but we have to walk in a *spirit of forgiveness* if we want to walk in the *power of His might*. Remember that His supernatural mediatorial power was released into the world when He prayed, "Father forgive...."

Are you looking for hope? Are you desperately seeking the missing link that will release you? Perhaps you realize you have been held in bondage, and now you are thinking, *I have also held other people in bondage. Now the armies of the enemy are encamped around me. How can I disperse them?*

The Holy Spirit is waiting to release you, *if you will forgive.* Don't let the excuses of your flesh or your mind distract you from what is most important right now.

I've been wronged. Who hasn't?

Life's dealt me a bad hand. So what? Join the club.

I was lied to. You're not the first one. You won't be the last one. Your Master was lied to. Are you any better than He is?

Those who were supposed to have been my friends forsook me. Join the club. Jesus is president. They all forsook Him and fled.

If you need help, ask God to help you forgive and release those people or circumstances that have hurt you. Ask Him to forgive you for every sin and failure in your life. He is faithful to forgive. He says, "The one who comes to Me I will by no means cast out" (Jn. 6:37b NKJV).

You were forgiven on Calvary, if you will only appropriate God's forgiveness. Do it now and experience the sweet release that comes when the God of Heaven forgives you once and for all. Do you doubt that you are a Christian? He says to you, *"Take up My cross and follow Me."* (See Mark 8:34.) It all begins with the same first step: Experience the power of divine forgiveness.

T.F. Tenney and Tommy Tenney – *Secret Sources of Power*

Reverence the Holy

hy were we so hesitant about things most of us had done thousands of times before? We were *amateurs at handling the holy.* (We still are!) I have noticed that early on in visitations of God's manifest presence, He comes suddenly and without warning. But in subsequent visitations, He comes only by invitation (displayed hunger). The crux of the whole matter is simple: Do you really want Him to come? Are you willing to pay the cost of becoming a God chaser? Then you will have to learn how to properly reverence, handle, and steward the holiness of God.

A.W. Tozer was deeply concerned about our loss of holiness in the Church. He noticed that the average church was losing that sense of sacredness in their worship services, and it grieved him. To him, that lack of reverence meant that people didn't think God's presence was in their church. (And it probably wasn't.) Tozer observed that the yearning and desiring of a spiritual life was losing out to worldly secularism. Such an environment does not produce revival. As a result, Tozer felt that God may actually look elsewhere if the Church does not come back to Him, to a relationship with *Him,* and not just His "stuff."

I now know why the high priests of old would say to their fellow priests, "Tie a rope around my ankle, because I'm going into the place where the glory of God abides. I've done everything I know to make myself ready, but I am in awe of God." I'm not afraid of God; I love Him. But I now have a respect for the glory and the holy things of God that I confess I didn't have before.

It used to be easy to handle the anointing, but now I know it is a sacred thing. Now I am careful to pray two things before I minister in most cases: I pray a prayer of thanksgiving first of all, saying, "Thank You, Lord, for visiting us." Then I ask the second part of that prayer, "Please stay, Lord."

If you remember the barren woman who prepared the prophet's room for Elijah in Second Kings chapter 4, she was rewarded with a son. When satan took him away in premature death, God sent the prophet to raise him back to life. Satan cannot steal what God has birthed, but God will only birth things *to people who make room for the miraculous* by faith. That is why I am careful to thank the Lord for coming, and then I tell Him that *we have made provisions for Him* to come again. "Lord, we're going to be here worshiping You on Wednesday, Thursday, and Friday. Our sole purpose is to praise Your name and seek Your lovely face." By faith I believe that God will visit us once again. I know from His Word that when God visits someone, He causes new and precious things to be born. And even if satan tries to kill them, God will move Heaven and earth to breathe life back into what He has birthed!

We need to learn how to handle the holy things of God with greater tenderness and sensitivity. We must remember that "the good" can quickly become the worst enemy of "the best." If you want God's best, then you will have to sacrifice what you think is good and acceptable. If you and I can find out what is acceptable to *Him*, "the best," then the promise of visitation becomes real.

I think I've seen a glimpse of what I think God is doing. *He is moving into position.*

Tommy Tenney – *The God Chasers*

Don't Take God for Granted

A lot of hungry church leaders today are reading everything they can find about past moves of God. Why? Because we are at the holy bump in the threshing floor. We somehow sense that if we really want the holiness of God and the fullness of His glory to dwell in our midst, then we need to find out how to properly handle the holy, God's glory. We know that this is where the flesh has to fall off, but what is God's way to do it? Our hunger is too deep for one meal to satisfy us. We are after more than His visitation. We want God's visitation to become a *habitation.* We want His *kabod,* not "Ichabod." We want His *present* presence to be here.

We are in the same situation as King David. Our greatest danger at this point is for *the sacred things to become common.* The ark of the covenant was housed in Abinadab's home for a long time, but God's presence was only there in a limited fashion. Some writers think Uzzah grew up around the ark of the covenant as a kid. Perhaps he played on it, sat on it, or swung his feet from the sides, and generally didn't think anything about it. If this is true, it was because God was there in a limited fashion.

However, when you start moving God's glory back to the place where it belongs, His "felt" or manifested presence and power will begin to be restored with every step back to His divine order. (Could the stumbling have come from the additional "weight" of the glory, the *kabod,* being restored to the ark?) You will no longer be able to get away with things that you used to take for granted. If we're not careful, we can allow sacred things to become so common that we begin to think like Uzzah: *I can touch it, see? I grew up with it; it's harmless.* We're going to touch God's glory one time too many.

Never take God's holy presence for granted, and never assume that if no one is crying, shaking, manifesting odd movements, or prophesying away, then God isn't at work. Be careful when you stifle a yawn of boredom and complacency. Many of the great saints in historic denominations and churches knew that God doesn't always have to manifest Himself in things seen by the eye of the flesh. They would solemnly warn all of us, "Don't come in here looking for sensationalism. Come looking for God and you will find Him."

We need to live with a new awareness of His constant presence. I want to be careful so it won't become so common to me that I begin to think I can casually reach out and touch His holiness with my flesh at any point. I want *Him* at any cost, and I will not let sacred things become common to me. If you are committed to participate in the visitation and habitation of God, then pray this with me:

"Lord God, I am here to meet with You, and I am learning how to handle the holy things of Your presence. Have mercy on me, Lord Jesus."

Tommy Tenney – *The God Chasers*

Can God Interrupt Your Schedule?

hink about all the "baggage" you carry around with you. Ask yourself, "Is all this necessary?" It may be legitimate, but it is still a weight, nonetheless. Schedules have become our slave-drivers and we have become "must do list" addicts! We are afraid to do anything or go anywhere without first checking our palm PCs, appointment books, electronic organizers, or on-line time management programs. Ask yourself: "Can God interrupt me? Have I made it impossible for the Almighty to get my attention without triggering a major catastrophe or sending fire down from Heaven?"

We need to stay open to divine interruption at any time. Some of the greatest "God experiences" in our lives can happen when we have something else planned. Pray that when God interrupts your schedule, you will be sensitive enough to realize it is God and obey Him rather than your appointment book! If you decide to pursue your own agenda instead of Him, don't be surprised if you "run into a brick wall" and wake up with a headache saying, "Oh, God. *What went wrong?*" His response will be simple, "You did. You went wrong when you didn't inquire of Me and seek My face."

The New Testament portrait of Mary and Martha responding to Jesus' visit to their home in Bethany reveals an important principle at work. Both of them were needed. Mary knew how to minister to the divinity of Christ, and she gave it top priority. Martha knew how to minister to His humanity and that was her primary focus. When you get both of these ministries operating in unity in the same house, there is power. Yet there must be balance.

Martha was so encumbered by her focus on ministry in the natural that she was blind to the priority of the spiritual. She made it difficult for the Spirit to interrupt her kitchen agenda of serving the Lord's natural needs for the sake of the spiritual. On the other hand, Mary was so "heavenly minded" that at times she bordered on the neglectful. If Martha hadn't been there, she would have kept Jesus talking long after dinnertime and into the night without a meal.

Forced to choose between the two, the Lord will always choose the one who sits at His feet in adoration and communes with Him. He will always put footwashers before food-preparers, but He prefers to have *both.* Somewhere in the middle of Martha's kitchen and Mary's seat of devotion at Jesus' feet there is a place of divine power. The ideal balance would place both.Mary and Martha at Jesus' feet in joyful devotion and communion until the appropriate time; then both would be released in power to serve Him and worship Him in the "kitchen" of life.

We must not be guilty of putting the secondary above the primary. Our primary purpose in life is to praise and worship God. We are called to be worshipers long before any of us are called to be "ministers of the gospel." (After we lay down our earthly bodies, we will lay down every secondary call, in order to praise and worship Him unceasingly.) It is possible to succeed in the secondary and fail in the primary, but this is not "true success" by eternity's measure.

All of us must deal with this balance between our primary "worship" calling and our secondary "ministry" calling. We never "graduate" from our worship ministry; we simply become qualified to carry an additional—and secondary—load from God.

T.F. Tenney and Tommy Tenney – *Secret Sources of Power*

We Have Lost the Art of Entertaining the Presence of God

We want to attract God's attention, but once we get Him to visit, or once we sense His presence settle down among us, we say, "Hi, glad You came—gotta go," and go on our way. Too often we want just enough of God in our place of worship to give us a tingle or make a little chill run up our spines. We say, "Oh, He's here." The question is, "Will He stay?" It's not about us; it is about Him.

There has to be more to it than thrills and chills. David wasn't content to have a temporary visitation. He was after more, and that was why he told the Levitical worshipers, "You are not going any-where. I want you and your group to take the first three hours. You guys take the next watch, and you take the third."

I long for the day when God's people will provide "24/7" worship to God, worshiping and honoring Him 24 hours a day, 7 days a week. With very few exceptions, church sanctuaries are the most unused rooms in America and around the world. While steady streams of people flock to 24-hour convenience stores to stock up on passing earthly needs, our churches can barely operate two hours per week because the demand for their "product" is so low. We must cultivate the lifestyle of "24/7" before launching organized structure lest it become like everything else we've done—*mechanical!*

I do not advocate artificially propping open the church doors. It is a call to the passion of the heart of David, a worshiper. *His tabernacle became God's favorite house because of who worshiped there!* Just as 114 Slack Street became my favorite house, not because of the magnolia tree or the white paint and green living room carpet, but because of who lived there—Mom and Dad and the family.

God just wants to be with His kids. Stables will do—it worked in Bethlehem and at Azusa Street. (The Azusa Street revival in Los Angeles was started in a converted stable.) Anything to get close. If David looked at his humble tabernacle and said, "Someday I hope to do better," then God answered, "A tent will do, David. Just keep your heart hot!"

We have built beautiful sanctuaries with hardly anyone inside because, if there is no flame, there is nothing to see. There is no *shekinah* glory in our churches because we have lost our ability to *host the Holy Ghost.* Why did God say that He would build David's house again? I believe that it is because David's tabernacle had no veil or walls of separation. He longs for intimacy between Himself and His people; He wants to reveal His glory to the lost and dying world. He has to rebuild it because the weak hands of man tired of holding open the gates of Heaven with their worship and intercession.

Are we willing to rediscover what David learned, or are we already bored with God's "heritage tour"?

I wonder what it meant to God to be able to sit in David's rustic tabernacle in all His glory, to be seated right in the midst of His people without any veils or walls separating Him from His creation for the first time since the garden.

Turn your face toward Him now and ask Him what He really wants. The answer will change you forever.

Tommy Tenney – *God's Favorite House*

Rediscovering the Manifest Presence of God

I don't know about you, my friend, but there's a driving passion in my heart that whispers to me that there's more than what I already know, more than what I already have. It makes me jealous of John, who wrote Revelation. It makes me envious of people who get glimpses out of *this* world into *that* world and see things that I only dream about. I know there's more. One reason I know there's more is because of those who have encountered the "more" and were never the same. God chasers! My prayer is, *I want to see You like John saw You!*

In all my reading and study of the Bible, I have never found any person mentioned in the Scriptures who really had a "God encounter" and then "backslid" and rebelled against God. Once you experience God in His glory, you can't turn away from Him or forget His touch. It's not just an argument or a doctrine; it's an *experience*. That is why the apostle Paul said, "...I know *whom* I have believed..." (2 Tim. 1:12). Unfortunately, many people in the Church would say, "I know *about* whom I have believed." That means they haven't met Him in His glory.

One reason people flow *out* the back doors of our churches as fast as they come in through the front door is because they have more of a "man encounter" with our programs than a "God encounter" with the unforgettable majesty and power of the Almighty God. What is needed are "Damascus road experiences" like Saul's encounter with God Himself. (See Acts 9:3-6.)

This speaks strongly of the difference between the *omnipresence* of God and the *manifest presence* of God. The phrase, "omnipresence of God," refers to the fact that He is everywhere all the time. He is that "particle" in the atomic nucleus that nuclear physicists cannot see and can only track. The Gospel of John touches on this quality of God when it says, "And without Him was not any thing made that was made" (Jn. 1:3b). God is everywhere in everything. He is the composite of everything, both the glue that holds the pieces of the universe together and the pieces themselves! This explains why people can sit on a bar stool in an inebriated state and suddenly feel the conviction of the Holy Spirit without the benefit of a preacher, gospel music, or any other Christian influence. God is literally right there in the bar with them, and the mind-numbing ability of alcohol to lower inhibitions also allows them to lose their inhibitions toward God. Unfortunately by then it is not always a "choice" of their will that moves them toward God, just the hunger of their hearts. Their "mind" is numb; their heart is hungry. When their "mind" recovers to discover the will is unbroken, they often revert because it was not a valid encounter. A hungry heart inside a man with an unbowed head (mind) and an unbroken (unsubmitted) will is a recipe for misery.

Now if God can do that in the bar room, why should we be surprised at all the other things He can do "all by Himself"? (Most people who don't come from a church background will tell you that the first time they felt the prick of the conviction of God was in some place *other* than in a church service or religious setting.) All these instances illustrate the effects of the omnipresence of God, the quality of His presence being everywhere, all the time.

Tommy Tenney – *The God Chasers*

Moses Wanted Habitation, Not Visitation

*T*he Israelites rarely took time to thank God for His mighty acts because they were too busy compiling "want lists" and official complaints connected with their physical and personal desires. The vast majority of us today have done the same thing. Moses, however, wanted something more. He had experienced the miracles. He had heard God's voice and witnessed His delivering power. More than any other person alive at that time, Moses had even experienced the manifest presence of God in measure, in temporary visitation. But everything he saw and experienced in God told him that there was *far more* just waiting for him beyond the cloud. He longed for more than *visitation*; his soul longed for *habitation*. He wanted more than just seeing God's finger or hearing His voice speaking from a cloud or a burning bush. He had gone beyond fear to love, and God's abiding presence had become his consuming desire. That is why he begged God in Exodus 33:18:

> *"I beseech Thee, show me Thy glory."*

He wanted to see God's face! God was quick to grant Moses' request for Israel. His presence would still go before the people, but He didn't grant Moses' most urgent request directly. First God said that He would cause all His goodness to pass before Moses, and that He knew Moses by name. But then the Lord explained to Moses, "Thou canst not see My face: for there shall no man see Me, and live"

(Ex. 33:20). That statement appears to be a closed case, but Moses somehow sensed "there was a way." The Lord told Moses, "Look, you can't see My face, but *there is a place by Me* where you can see Me as I disappear off in the distance" (see Ex. 33:21-23).

Most people would have been more than happy with that answer, but Moses had tasted the unearthly joy of the Lord's presence and he was acquiring a taste for God that couldn't be satisfied from a "safe" distance. A hunger had been ignited in his being that would drive him to risk death in God's presence to achieve satisfaction. That hunger was destined to span 1,500 years and death itself to find fulfillment.

The Lord told Moses to "present himself" to Him on top of the mountain the next morning, and He would hide him in the cleft of a rock while His glory passed by. Now that is an interesting procedure. God was saying, "Now before I ever get there, I am going to reach forward in time to cover you with My hand while I pass by you. After I pass by, I am going to pull My hand away so you can stick your head out and look in the direction I've gone. Then you will see just a little bit of My 'back parts' as I disappear into the distance" (see Ex. 33:22-23).

So God came in His glory at the speed of light or faster to proclaim His divine name and pass by in His glory. As He passed by, He pulled His hand away from the cleft in the rock so Moses could see the backside of His glory disappearing in the distance. Even though this brief revelation came as quickly as a flash of lightning, it made such an impact on Moses that he was able to dictate the Book of Genesis for later generations, the "backside" or the history of God, describing his vision of the creation.

Tommy Tenney – *The God Chasers*

Guided by the Eye of God

Too often God's people can be guided only by the written Word or the prophetic word. The Bible says He wants us to move beyond that to a place marked by a greater degree of tenderness of heart toward Him and by a deeper maturity that allows Him to "guide us with His eye" (see Ps. 32:8-9). In the kind of home in which I was raised, my mom or dad could just look at me a certain way and get the job done. If I was straying down the path of childhood foolishness, they didn't always have to say anything. Just the look in their eyes as they glanced or glared toward me would give me the guidance that I needed. Do you still *need* to hear a thundering voice from behind the pulpit? A biting prophetic utterance to correct your ways? Or are you able to read the emotion of God on His face? Are you tenderhearted enough that His eye can guide you and convict your heart of sin? When He glances your way, are you quick to say, "Oh, I can't do that. I can't go there, and I can't say that because it would displease my Father"? The glance of God convicted Peter, and to the altar music of a rooster crowing he wept his way to tenderness.

God is everywhere, but *He doesn't turn His face and His favor everywhere.* That is why He tells us to seek His face. Yes, He is present with you every time you meet with other believers in a worship service, but how long has it been since your hunger caused you to crawl up in His lap, and like a child, to reach up and take the face of God to turn it toward you? Intimacy with Him! That is what God desires, and His face should be our highest focus.

The Israelites referred to the manifest presence of God as the *shekinah* glory of God. When David began to talk about bringing the ark of the covenant back to Jerusalem, he wasn't interested in the gold-covered box with the artifacts inside it. He was interested in the blue flame that hovered between the outstretched wings of the cherubim on top of the ark. That is what he wanted, because there was something about the flame that signified that God Himself was present. And wherever that glory or manifested presence of God went, there was victory, power, and blessing. Intimacy will bring about "blessing," but the pursuit of "blessing" won't always bring about intimacy.

What we cry for is a restoration of the manifested presence of God. When Moses was exposed to the glory of God, the residue of that glory caused his face to shine so much that when he came back down from the mountain, the people said, "Moses, you must cover your face. We can't bear to look at you" (see Ex. 34:29-35). Whatever or whoever is exposed to the manifested presence of God begins to absorb the very material matter of God. Can you imagine what it was like in the Holy of Holies? How much of the glory of God had been absorbed by those badger skins, the veil, and the ark itself?

Tommy Tenney – *The God Chasers*

Called to
"A Place in Him"

The sad and unfortunate truth of the Book of Exodus is that the motley group of people God brought to Mount Sinai was *not the group of people* that He took across the river Jordan into the promised land. *Something happened at the mountain.* God called them and made them a nation for the first time in their history. He called them to a place—a place of blessing and a place of change— where they didn't want to go. Don't fall into the trap of thinking that this "place" was merely some physical spot on the map, because these people were already traipsing across the wilderness. Their blessing didn't consist of some rocky real estate someplace, although the promised land was part of the package deal. God called them to *a promised place in Him.* He called them to a place of covenant, a place of intimacy with their Creator that was not offered to any other people on the planet at that time. *That's the secret of the secret place.* We think that the idea of a "kingdom of priests" is an exclusively New Testament or Christian idea, but it was also God's original plan for Israel!

> *And the Lord said unto Moses, Go unto the people, and sanctify them to day and to morrow, and let them wash their clothes,*
>
> *And be ready against the third day: for the third day the Lord will come down in the sight of all the people upon mount Sinai.*
>
> *...when the trumpet soundeth long, they shall come up to the mount* (Exodus 19:10-11,13b).

Although the first generation of Israelites gathered around the mountain would ultimately believe the fearful spies and shrink away from the promised land in fear, the real cause of their failure is found right there at the foot of Mount Sinai. God intended for *all* the Israelites to come *close to Him* on the mountain, but they were uncomfortable.

> *And all the people saw the thunderings, and the lightnings, and the noise of the trumpet, and the mountain smoking: and when the people saw it,* **they removed, and stood afar off.**
>
> *And they said unto Moses, Speak thou with us, and we will hear: but* **let not God speak with us, lest we die.**
>
> *And Moses said unto the people, Fear not: for God is come to prove you, and that His fear may be before your faces, that ye sin not.*
>
> *And the* **people stood afar off,** *and* **Moses drew near** *unto the thick darkness where God was* (Exodus 20:18-21).

They saw the lightning and heard the thunder, and they shrank back in fear. They ran from His presence instead of pursuing Him as Moses did. They were unhappy with the style of leadership that God had chosen. (He couldn't lay down His identity as the Almighty God just to please man then, and He won't do it today either.) So the end result of their flight from holy intimacy that day was that they died before they or their children ever entered the promised land. *They preferred distant respect over intimate relationship.*

It wasn't God's original plan for the first generation of Israelites to die in the wilderness. He wanted to take the *same group* of people whom He brought out of the land of bondage into the land of promise. He wanted to give His new nation of former slaves their very own land and inheritance, but they wouldn't have it because of fear and unbelief. Their doom was sealed when they looked across the Jordan at the promised land and shrank back, but it really began when they shrank back from God's presence in the cloud on Mount Sinai. It was there that they ran from God and demanded that Moses stand between them. (The Church has been suffering from the same problem ever since.) We often prefer that a man stand between us and God. We have a hell-inspired, fleshly fear of holy intimacy with God. The roots of this fear reach all the way back to the Garden of Eden. Adam and Eve hid in shameful fear while God longed for sweet fellowship.

Tommy Tenney – *The God Chasers*

Set Christ Before You and Endure

Now He wants us to remember Him as we face the contradictions and challenges of life. This is the way to endure and not grow weary or fainthearted. The Bible says that when Jesus endured the cross, He did it "for the joy that was set before Him..." (Heb. 12:2b NKJV). His joy was at least twofold: He anticipated the joy of pleasing His Father, and He anticipated the joy of seeing millions of lost people coming into the Kingdom of God.

Frustration over things you don't understand can quickly weigh you down. We serve a God who speaks worlds into existence with a single command. He is not prone to providing explanations for the endless questions we send His way. If it isn't in His Word already, and if He doesn't answer a question through His Spirit, we are left with an unanswered "why" to deal with. David asks "why" at least 29 times in the *New King James Version* of the Psalms, and God called him "a man after My own heart, who will do all My will" (Acts 13:22b NKJV). Be encouraged: You are not the first individual whose mind is filled with "whys." The biggest room in your brain should be reserved for "Things I Do Not Understand."

Sometimes you have to "unload" some weight before you can take on any more. Life gets difficult when we give too much "weight" to the things we cannot change in life. The first thing we should do is make sure we aren't carrying the weight of any sin in our lives.

The redemptive blood of Jesus Christ cleanses us from all sin. Even though we want to lay aside every weight, we sometimes fail to comprehend God's power to forget. In other words, we carry the effects of sin with us when technically, they are no longer ours to bear. Once we cast them into the "sea of forgetfulness," they are only as effective in our lives as we allow them to be. We must accept God's full forgiveness and lay aside our sins and failures forever.

If the enemy cannot ensnare you in an overt or illegitimate way by tempting you to commit some sin of commission, then he will try to ensnare you in a "legitimate" way—through sins of *omission*. Either way, we take care of sins through repentance. Someone once boasted to me, "I don't need to repent!" My response to him was, "You need to repent for feeling like you don't need to repent!"

T.F. Tenney and Tommy Tenney – *Secret Sources of Power*

God Doesn't Dare Come Any Closer...

M ost of us are content to preserve some bit of our fallen life or fleshly ambitions while lightly clinging to the hem of God's garment of salvation. Oh, we can cling to the remnants of "our own thing" as long as we are willing to live on the handouts God is able to give us when He sticks His hand out from under the veil. It is only enough to keep us from spiritual famine, but God doesn't dare come any closer because it would kill the very flesh we prize so highly. The choice is ours.

God is looking for someone who is willing to tie a rope around an ankle and say, "If I perish, I perish; but I am going to see the King. I want to do everything I can to go behind that veil. I'm going to put on the blood, I'm going to repent, I'm going to do everything I can because I'm tired of knowing *about* Him. *I want to know Him. I've got to see His face.*"

No matter who you are, what you've done, or what religious tradition you embrace; the only way you are going to go through that veil is through the death of your flesh. The death of genuine repentance and brokenness before God will allow Him to draw near to you. The apostle Paul said, "For now we see through a glass, darkly; but then *face to face:* now I know in part; but then shall I know even as also I am known" (1 Cor. 13:12). At that point we will know God in the full measure of who He is, the way He knows us in the full measure of who we are.

The apostle John was exiled to the prison island of Patmos because of his faith in Christ, but I'm convinced there was a deeper reason for it. It was only after John was a walking dead man abandoned on a deserted island to die that he heard a voice and turned to look in the face of God the Son, Jesus Christ.

We all think we've known God and we all think we've been a part of the Church. But we need to look closely at John. This was the apostle who personally leaned on the breast of Jesus. He was the closest disciple. John watched Jesus awaken from a sound sleep to calm the storm on the Sea of Galilee. He saw Jesus literally stop a funeral procession to touch the body of a dead boy, raise him from the dead, and restore him to his mother. Yet this same apostle turned around on the island of Patmos and *saw Him* in His unveiled glory for the first time. He said that the Lord's head and hair were white like wool, and His eyes burned like fire. His feet were like fine brass. The Scriptures say that John fell at the Lord's feet *as though he were dead* (see Rev. 1:17). Why would John do that when he had already known Jesus for three years? In the visionary instant that John saw Him, he tasted death because he had seen life. It takes death to really see Him, and all I can say is, "It's a good day to die." The more I die, the closer He gets.

John the Baptist knew that secret too. Jesus said, "...Among them that are born of women there hath not risen a greater than John the Baptist" (Mt. 11:11a). Why? John had the grace to understand the little-known principle upon which all true ministry, service, and worship stand:

He must increase, but I must decrease (John 3:30).

If I decrease, then He can increase. Less of me means more of Him. John the Baptist was wise enough to acknowledge the true Giver of all gifts and abilities. He said, "A man can receive nothing, except it be given him from heaven" (Jn. 3:27b). Basically, if there is less of me, then there is room for more of Him. The more of me that dies, the closer He can get. How far can this go? Well, I don't know, but I can tell you the name of somebody to ask. Check with Enoch. He showed us that you can literally walk with God, but you will "die" along the way.

The Bible says, "And they overcame him by the blood of the Lamb, and by the word of their testimony; and they loved not their lives unto the death" (Rev. 12:11). Are you avoiding death? Do you want God's blessings on your life? The greatest blessing doesn't come from God's hand; it comes from His face in intimate relationship. When you finally see Him and know Him, you have come to the source of all power.

Tommy Tenney – *The God Chasers*

Daddy, You Can Sit Anywhere You Want

One time I was away from home when I called to talk to my youngest daughter, Andrea. I said, "What are you doing, baby girl?" She said, "I'm playing tea party, Daddy." I told her, "Set a place for me right now, and we'll just pretend that I'm there and we'll have tea." "I already did," she replied. "Well, where am I sitting?" I asked, and she said, "Well, I didn't know, so I set five places for you." That melted my heart!

How long has it been since the Church was so desperate for Him that we just said, "Father, You can sit anywhere You want. Here, there, it doesn't matter. Just come." I answered my daughter, "When I get home, Daddy is going to play tea party with you."

All this took place in the middle of the summer in Louisiana when the temperature hits 95 degrees in the shade with 95 percent humidity. Andrea's little plastic playhouse was in the backyard, right in the hot sun. The minute I walked in the door with suitcases in hand, Andrea was saying, "Come on, Daddy." I hadn't even unpacked, but I had a promise to keep. *It was time for Daddy to go play tea party.*

Her playhouse was so small I'm not sure whether I got in it or put it on! My head was holding up the roof while I sat on the ground. I was barely crammed in Andrea's little playhouse before she had handed me a tiny apron with the command, "Put it on." She had the table set and waiting for me, and we started drinking our imaginary tea. She picked up one cup and said, "Here, Daddy." Then she went around the table, "Here, dolly, and this is for me." Then we sat and "supped" together. Andrea asked me, "Is it good?"

"Oh yes, it's good," I told her, even though we were sweating bullets in the hot sun, sipping imaginary tea. Then Andrea said, "Here, have some cookies." (*They were imaginary cookies.*) Once again, she asked, "Is this fun?" The truth of the matter was that I was miserable, but I was with her, and therefore it was fun. So I said, "Yes, baby, it's fun."

Finally Andrea said, "Daddy, it's hot and I'm thirsty. Let's go in the big house and get something to drink." I said, "Come on, baby," and I took her into the big house and sat her down at the real table. I poured some real iced tea in the glasses and sat there with her. Then she said to me, "*Now this is a real tea party.*"

We've been playing tea party in our plastic houses too, only we call it "having church." We are forcing God to be confined within the constraints of our playhouse structures while feeding Him make-believe worship and praise. Then we look at Him and say, "Aren't we having fun?"

Tommy Tenney – *God's Favorite House*

The Secret Path to His Presence

"**I** know it's here somewhere; I can tell I'm close. There has got to be a way to get in there. Oh, there it is. This path doesn't look really nice, though. In fact, it's kind of broken and bloody. Let's see what they call this path... Repentance. Are you sure this is the way? Are you sure this is how I can reach my goal of His face and His presence? I'm going to ask a fellow traveler. Moses, what do you say? You've been there; tell me."

> And the Lord said unto Moses, I will do this thing also that thou hast spoken: for thou hast found grace in My sight, and I know thee by name.
>
> And he said, I beseech Thee, **show me Thy glory**.
>
> And He said, Thou canst not see My face: for **there shall no man see Me, and live** (Exodus 33:17-18,20).

When Moses asked God to show him His glory, the Lord warned him that no man can see Him and live. Even in the new covenant, this statement is true. Only dead men can see God. There *is* a connection between His glory and our death.

When Moses began to press the case with God and said, "I want to, I've got to," Moses already had the outline of the tabernacle. He was the man God chose to receive the architectural details of the pre-Calvary model of salvation and man's ultimate restoration to His presence. I am positive that Moses looked at the tabernacle and the law and thought, *This is not really it; this is just some sort of a model of what God is going to do. It's only a type, a shadow.* I think he knew that the furniture and utensils of the tabernacle all had symbolic meaning. He wanted to see the finished product. This man "started a cathedral" that was too big to build in one generation, so he said, "Show me Your glory." That was when the Lord said, "You can't. Only dead men can see My face."

That's why I love to read about the visionary prayers of people like Aimee Semple McPherson and William Seymour who used to stick his head in an apple crate during all-night prayer meetings on Azusa Street and pray for the glory of God to come down. I believe that when the conglomerate prayers of God's people gather together and finally reach a crescendo of power, hunger, and intensity, it finally gets to be "too much" for God to delay any longer. At that point He finally says, "That's it. I won't wait any longer. It is time!"

That is what happened in Argentina in the 1950's. A man named Edward Miller wrote a book entitled, *Cry for Me Argentina*, in which he describes one of the origins of the great revival in Argentina that was destined to impact South America and ultimately the entire world. Dr. Miller is now in his eighties, but more than four decades earlier he was one of but a few Pentecostal or Full Gospel missionaries working in Argentina. He tells the story of how 50 students in his Argentine Bible Institute began to pray and had an angelic visitation. They had to suspend classes because of the heavy prayer burden they had for the nation of Argentina. Day after day for 49 days in a row, these students prayed and interceded for Argentina in this Bible school. Argentina was a spiritual wasteland at the time, as far as Dr. Miller knew. He said he only knew of 600 Spirit-filled believers in the entire nation during those years under the government of Juan Peron.

Dr. Miller told me that he had never seen people weep so hard and so long in prayer. It had to be supernatural in origin and purpose. We don't know much about interceding today. Many of us think it consists of screaming against evil spirits, but that's not what needs to happen. We simply need for "Father" to show up.

Tommy Tenney – *The God Chasers*

His Mercy Keeps Him Away From Us

t is God's *mercy* that keeps Him away from us. For generation after generation, Christians have prayed strange little prayers and beat the altars saying, "God come near, God come near." I believe He has been answering us all along, but with a doubled-edged answer. With one hand, He beckons on, calling out to us, "Come on, call Me closer and I will come because I want to come near." Yet at the same time, He holds out His other hand in warning while saying, "Be careful, be careful. If you're going to get any closer, then make sure that everything is dead. If you really want to know Me, then everything must die."

Why did God audience death? What was it about the stench of the burning hair and hide of a sacrifice that was so inviting to God that it caused Him to literally leave Heaven and visit the place of a burning sacrifice? There is something about death that is inviting to God. You may not realize it, but death has been in every revival in Church history! Death was there in those early meetings on Azusa Street. Death was there in the First and Second Great Awakenings. The Pentecostal pioneer, Frank Bartleman, of the Azusa revival, said, "The depth of your repentance will determine the height of your revival."

The more death that God smells,

the closer He can come.

It's as if the smell of that sacrifice was a signal that God could draw near to His people for a moment without striking them down for their sin. His end goal has always been reunion and intimate communion with mankind, His highest creation; but sin made that a fatal affair. God cannot come close to living flesh because it reeks of the world. It has to be dead flesh for Him to come close. So when we beg for God to come close, He will, but He also says, "I can't really get any closer, because if I do, your flesh will be destroyed. I want you to understand that if you will just go ahead and die, then I can come near to you."

That is why repentance and brokenness—the New Testament equivalent of death—brings the manifest presence of God so near. But we want to avoid repentance because we don't like the smell of death. Anyone who has ever smelled the obnoxious odor of burning hair and hide will agree that it doesn't smell good. It isn't enticing to the senses of mankind, but it is very enticing to God because it is a signal that He can once again draw close to those He loves.

Tommy Tenney – *The God Chasers*

Can People Tell You Have Been With Jesus?

How long has it been since you were excited about Jesus? Has the glory of God shone through your personal presence recently? Can people feel your presence and marvel that "you've been with Jesus"? (See Acts 4:13.) We know this happens. By the same token, they can also tell when we have *not* been with Him.

It is too easy for us to bow our knees and not bow our hearts. We cross our fingers behind our backs and pretend that God doesn't see through our performance while we confess total love and loyalty with less-than-total sincerity. The problem is that total relinquishment does not come without a price (and we tend to avoid commitments that require a payment). In God's Kingdom, it is a price worth paying *for there is power with relinquishment.*

You are not a real soldier until you've endured the pain, the discipline, the breaking and remaking that comes in boot camp of relinquishment. The discipline of relinquishment even follows us onto the battlefield at times.

Several years ago a preacher said that the Lord spoke to him during a time of prayer and said:

"*I have seen your ministry. Would you like to see Mine?*"

The preacher said, "Yes, Lord. What do I have to do?"

God said, "*Give Me back My church.*"

The pastor said, "Lord, it *is* Your church."

God replied, "*No. You control everything that is in it. You set the time when the service starts and you dictate when it ends. Worst of all, you control everything in between. I have even heard you call it 'my church.'* "

The pastor repented before the Lord and said, "Lord, it is not my church; it is Your church. I want Your ministry. My ministry at its best is not sufficient at all. I want to see what You can do because what I can do will not get the job done."

The stupidity of independence is as old as Adam and Eve. We must realize that we could not even breathe one breath, think one thought, or earn one dime without His blessing and empowerment. Anything less is presumption and rebellion. *The very taproot of rebellion is in the desire to be "great" on our own terms.* God's treatment and cure for the spirit of independence and rebellion in a believer is the discipline of relinquishment.

Anyone aspiring to leadership in God's Kingdom must learn how to relinquish man's "stability" and embrace God's change, for He is constantly transforming His people in preparation for the great wedding supper of the Lamb. That means change will be our constant companion. Where there is change, there must be relinquishment.

T.F. Tenney and Tommy Tenney – *Secret Sources of Power*

A Chance to Meet the One You Always Knew Was There

Whenever I encounter a party scene or see people drinking and acting like pure pagans, *I can't help but like them!* They don't play any religious games. They know who and what they are. (The ones who irritate me are the ones who play games and pretend to be something they are not!) Almost every time I pass by a bar or nightclub, the crazy thought comes to mind, *Lord, why not right here? Why don't You just break out right here?*

My definition of revival is when God's glory breaks out of the four walls of our churches to flow through the streets of the city. Revival of historical proportions in modern times would be when God invades the shopping malls on Friday night. I want to see every mall association be forced to hire full-time chaplains just to handle the crowds of people they find weeping under conviction each shopping day. I want to see citywide calls for volunteer ministers just to handle the flood of people who get convicted of their sins when they pass through the town. (Security guards know what to do with shoplifters, but would they know what to do with people who come up to them in distress because they've been convicted of their sin?) Hasten the day!

I believe God has stirred such a pent-up demand for His presence that in the "day of the Lord" (if His people will pursue His presence), the existing churches will not be able to handle the explosion of lost souls wanting to be saved. The modern Church is a caretaker or a maintenance organization at best, and a museum of what once was, at worst. Our greatest problem is that we've "stocked our shelves" with the wrong stuff. We offer the hungry our dusty shelves of bland, man-produced religious ritual that no one in his right mind is really hungry for! Empty religious ritual is as appetizing as "blue mashed potatoes" or some other unnatural concoction. If anybody could ever open a store that just dispenses Jesus, the hungry masses would come. Perhaps the reason we haven't stocked our services with the right stuff is because it doesn't come cheap.

The Church today has made it to the halfway point in its journey across the wilderness. We are camped at the foot of Mount Sinai, much like the children of Israel in the Book of Exodus. It is obvious that we have reached the point where we are going to have to make a decision. Will we go in or run away?

> *And Moses went up unto God, and the Lord called unto him out of the mountain, saying, Thus shalt thou say to the house of Jacob, and tell the children of Israel;*
>
> *Ye have seen what I did unto the Egyptians, and how I bare you on eagles' wings, and brought you unto Myself.*
>
> *Now therefore, if ye will obey My voice indeed, and keep My covenant, then ye shall be a peculiar treasure unto Me above all people: for all the earth is Mine:*
>
> *And **ye shall be unto Me a kingdom of priests, and an holy nation**. These are the words which thou shalt speak unto the children of Israel* (Exodus 19:3-6).

This is New Testament language on the pages of the Old Testament. They were given the obvious option of leap-frogging to a new level of intimacy. (See 1 Peter 2:9.)

Tommy Tenney – *The God Chasers*

Sit in the Lap of the Blesser

G od is saying to us, "I have set before thee an open door" (see Rev. 3:7-13). This is one of those seasons when God seems to be throwing open the door of Heaven and saying, "Come in to a new place of intimacy and communion with Me." You don't need to worry about the blessings if you sit in the lap of the Blesser! Just tell Him that you love Him and every blessing you ever imagined will come to you. Seek the Blesser, not the blessing! Seek the Reviver, not revival! Seek His face, not His hands!

Often I see the aisles of churches strewn with people who have climbed into the lap of the Father. I see them hiding their faces underneath benches and pews as they seek the face of God. Something is happening in the Church today, and it has nothing to do with the hype and manipulation of man. Aren't you sick of all that? Aren't you hungry for an encounter with God that's not contaminated by the vain promotions and manipulations of fleshly leaders? Don't you long to have God just introduce Himself to you? You are not alone. There was one woman who marked the road of repentance with her tears and *dismantled her glory* for the Lord.

And one of the Pharisees desired Him that He would eat with him. And He went into the Pharisee's house, and sat down to meat.

And, behold, a woman in the city, which was a sinner, when she knew that Jesus sat at meat in the Pharisee's house, brought an alabaster box of ointment,

And stood at His feet behind Him weeping, and began to wash His feet with tears, and did wipe them with the hairs of her head, and kissed His feet, and anointed them with the ointment.

Now when the Pharisee which had bidden Him saw it, he spake within himself, saying, This man, if He were a prophet, would have known who and what manner of woman this is that toucheth Him: for she is a sinner.

And Jesus answering said unto him, Simon, I have somewhat to say unto thee. And he saith, Master, say on.

There was a certain creditor which had two debtors: the one owed five hundred pence, and the other fifty.

And when they had nothing to pay, he frankly forgave them both. Tell Me therefore, which of them will love him most?

Simon answered and said, I suppose that he, to whom he forgave most. And He said unto him, Thou hast rightly judged.

And He turned to the woman, and said unto Simon, Seest thou this woman? I entered into thine house, thou gavest Me no water for My feet: but she hath washed My feet with tears, and wiped them with the hairs of her head.

Thou gavest Me no kiss: but this woman since the time I came in hath not ceased to kiss My feet.

My head with oil thou didst not anoint: but this woman hath anointed My feet with ointment.

Wherefore I say unto thee, Her sins, which are many, are forgiven; for she loved much: but to whom little is forgiven, the same loveth little.

And He said unto her, Thy sins are forgiven.

And they that sat at meat with Him began to say within themselves, Who is this that forgiveth sins also?

And He said to the woman, Thy faith hath saved thee; go in peace (Luke 7:36-50).

You may be only a few spiritual inches away from the encounter of a lifetime. If you want to see the face of God, then just follow Mary to the feet of Jesus. Pull out your alabaster box of precious sacrificial praise and worship. You've been holding your treasure back for too long, but there is One here who is worthy of it all. Don't hold anything back!

The Gospels of Matthew and Mark also record this event, and they say that Simon was or had been a leper. (See Matthew 26:6-7; Mark 14:3.) Many scholars believe that the account recorded by Dr. Luke is the story of an earlier event, but even so, Simon the Pharisee was *still* a spiritual leper because he was afflicted with the disfiguring sin of hypocrisy. You can always count on some Pharisees with the leprosy of hypocrisy showing up to look with disdain as you rush in to throw your best at the Lord's feet, but who cares? Who knows what problems will be lifted from your shoulders in that moment? Who knows what worries, fears, and anxieties will fade away when you hear Him say, "I accept you."

In God's eyes, we are all lepers in the spirit realm. We need to be those who return to the One who delivered us to offer thanksgiving. God's acceptance means you can ignore all the other voices that say, "I reject you." I don't mean to be rude, but who cares how many other lepers reject you when you have been healed and accepted by the King?

In the Gospels of Matthew and Mark, Mary's harshest critics weren't the Pharisees or Sadducees. The disciples of Jesus were ready to throw her out when Jesus quickly intervened.

> *And Jesus said,* **Let her alone***; why trouble ye her? she hath wrought a good work on Me.*
>
> *She hath done what she could: she is come aforehand to anoint My body to the burying.*
>
> *Verily I say unto you, Wheresoever this gospel shall be preached throughout the whole world, this also that she hath done shall be spoken of for a memorial of her (Mark 14:6,8-9).*

Tommy Tenney – The God Chasers

What Is an Open Heaven?

hat do I mean when I talk about an "open Heaven"? An "open Heaven" is *a place of easy access to God.* We know from Paul's writings that there are at least three "heavens." He told the church at Corinth that he was once "caught up to the third heaven." (See 2 Corinthians 12:2-4.) If there is a third heaven, of necessity there must be a second and a first heaven. The third heaven can only be the domain of God and His holy angels. It is the realm and "residence" of God. His rule from the third heaven affects the other heavens beneath it.

Since the Bible describes satan as "the prince of the power of the air," the second heaven is the dominion of the demonic. (See Ephesians 2:2.) The first heaven refers to the natural "sky" over our heads and the general dominion of man, or all that is within man's reach. Chapter 10 in the Book of Daniel provides a clear picture of all three heavens in dynamic conflict. When Daniel prayed to God from the first heaven, celestial conflict broke out in the second heaven between Michael the archangel and the fallen angelic ruler called the prince of Persia. God's answer to Daniel's prayer came through despite every effort in the dark realm to hinder or delay it. *Remember, delay is not denial.* Persistence plays a powerful role in opening Heaven. What if Daniel had stopped praying after 18 days or 20 days? You must not let "brass heavens" deter you!

When we use the term "brass heavens," we are not saying that God cannot hear our prayers. (See Deuteronomy 28:23.) He heard Daniel's prayer and instantly dispatched an angel with His answer.

The problem is that this angel passed through the second heaven where satan sent his own fallen angels to disrupt the communication. The adversary will try to stop your prayer from going up to God, and he will try to hinder the delivery of God's answer to you as well because the second heaven is his domain—*for now.*

Paul described satan as the "prince of the power of the air" in Ephesians 2:2. The adversary doesn't have complete dominion over the second heaven; he has limited dominion. He is only a created being and a fallen angelic prince. He can't even be compared to the eternal God and risen King. *A prince only has the power delegated to him by the king.* Our God has all power; satan the fallen prince only has the authority released to him by the King. There will come a day when even that authority will be stripped from him. Jesus has already stripped satan of the keys to hell and death. (See Revelation 1:18.) *Satan doesn't even have the keys to his own "house"!* But he still has the "house." On that great day, God is coming to go one step further by "repossessing the house."

Do you want to see the windows of Heaven open up? Besides the biblical characters and their experiences, heroic figures from Church history also have left clues about opening Heaven. John Bunyan is one of them. His classic allegory, *Pilgrim's Progress*, may be the best known Christian book ever written, yet Bunyan didn't consider it to be his best book. His choice was a short book entitled, *The Acceptable Sacrifice*, which he wrote late in his life. It is a book about brokenness based on an anointed exegesis of Psalm 51. Bunyan died while it was being printed, but he said that the book was "the culmination of my life's work." It was in Psalm 51 that David declared, *"The sacrifices of God are a broken spirit: a broken and a contrite heart, O God, Thou wilt not despise"* (Ps. 51:17). This is **the costly key that unlocks the riches of God's presence!** This is the fragrance God cannot ignore. He will respond. The brass heavens will be broken!

Tommy Tenney – *God's Favorite House*

Finding Favor

I wish you could see my youngest daughter's room. There are entire toy stores that don't carry as much variety as what is contained in that relatively small space!

Many of these "treasures" are acquired while we're traveling together. We can hardly pass a store anymore that one of my girls doesn't want to visit—and once inside, we can hardly leave without one of them finding a little something that they just can't live without! It isn't fair, really; I'm helpless against their advances. All they need to do is look up at me with their big, puppy dog eyes and say, "Pleeeeeeeeeeeeeeeeease!"

Within reason...I usually give in. (My wife may argue, though, over my definition of "within reason"!) And for a few golden moments all is well in the world. I am showered with hugs and kisses, treated to ear-to-ear smiles, and praised as "*the bestest daddy*" that ever was.

But these moments are fleeting! Soon the smiles fade into wistful longings again as the *next* desirable object comes into view. And I'm left *literally* holding the bag as they examine their next prospective purchase!

I can say all that with a smile on my face because I'm not trying to buy my family's affections. Our love for each other has been tested and proven through the good times and the bad. We've had times of plenty...and plenty of times of scarcity! We've come to understand that the best things we can give to each other are ourselves—and that is priceless. Like all good fathers, I hope that my family never has to return to the "hard times." Yet I can't help but look back on those times with a degree of fondness, because the strongest bonds are always forged in adversity. I never want to go back through some things again, but I wouldn't give anything for the lessons I learned in them.

I respond to my girls because of my relationship with them. If someone else's little girl were to follow me around all day, asking me to buy her just about everything in sight, my response would be quite different. She could be a perfect child, talented and charming; she could have the "puppy dog eyes" down pat, but her pleas wouldn't move me. It isn't that I lack the ability to grant her request—but she isn't my daughter! My daughters have my *favor* in a way that no one else's children will ever have.

Now, that doesn't mean that my kids always get what they want from me; nor does it mean that they'll get it on their timetable! (Well, my wife may argue that point too....) But the depth of our relationship is such that their love for me isn't affected by the little disappointments that all families must face along the way.

We're God's children, and as His kids we have access to His favor in much the same way that my kids have access to mine. His Fatherly love for us is unconditional—but our childlike faith and love for Him isn't always where it should be. Sometimes we'll pout and refuse to receive His love when we don't get our way. And even when we *do* get our way, our love for Him can be shallow.

Too often we run from blessing to blessing, pleading with God to dispense His gifts...and almost as soon as we have them, we turn our attention from Him and look longingly at the next "thing" that catches our eye, rubbing our hands together in presumptive anticipation of the next blessing. And to some extent God will overlook our immaturity— if we've proven that our love for Him is deeper than our love for His "things." Sometimes we think that it is enough to "come as a child." We have to come as *His* child, His "babes and sucklings" (see Mt. 21:16). Otherwise, we're just *acting childish*...or worse than that, as impostors!

Children depend on their parents for everything: food, shelter, toys, and a lot of love and companionship. My most precious moments with my children aren't when they're excited and thanking me for getting them some new toy. The moments I crave the most are when they drop their toys, forget about their "wish list," and climb up into my lap for no reason in particular—just to love me and be with me. In those moments, nothing else matters. I'll drop whatever I'm doing and give them my full attention. *God longs for those moments with His kids too!*

"God comes to earth because His growling hunger pains for worship draw Him to the imperfect praise of His children, who say, "*I luv You, Daddy.*" He isn't particularly impressed with our polished singing and multimillion-dollar buildings. It is all pitiful by celestial standards, but it is precious to Him because He loves us.

" '*Red and yellow, black and white,*

They are precious in His sight.

*Jesus loves the **little** children of the world.'*

"*He comes because we hold up childlike imperfect praise with hearts full of love*—like a child reaching up and a Father reaching down" (Tommy Tenney, *God's Favorite House* [Shippensburg, PA: Fresh Bread, 1999], 117).

There's an irony in the way God operates. When we're grabbing for the gifts from His hands, He seems to dispense them slowly. But when we get our eyes off of the "toys" and onto His face—when we want Him, regardless of the blessings *and regardless of the cost*—that is when He lavishes His gifts upon us.

If you want His favor, seek His face. Gifts of His hands are wonderful, but they are temporary things. They'll never really satisfy. But when we come to Him as His children in worship and adoration, we're building on a firm foundation: the face of our Father, the only One whose favor really matters in the end. As Andre Crouch recently wrote (in a song inspired by *The God Chasers*), "All of the gifts from Your hands could never replace Your face."

GodChasers.network newsletter

I Am Tired of Racing to False Finish Lines

I t is no longer acceptable merely to have some good services, good music, and good preaching. We must meet God Himself. I am so weary of "almost" services that at times I tell people in our meetings, "If you came here for some good meetings, you've got the wrong model, the wrong preacher, the wrong place, and the wrong day. Come back another day. But if what you are after is God, then welcome to the brotherhood of the burning heart."

It was to the lukewarm church of Laodicea that Jesus said, "Behold, I stand at the door, and knock: if any man hear My voice, and open the door, I will come in to him..." (Rev. 3:20). *The Holy Spirit is shopping for the place of the next outbreak.* He is standing at the front door of our churches looking for someone like David who has prepared a place for His weighty habitation—a place where worshipers are willing to prop open the door of Heaven with their upraised hands so His glory can come down and stay among them.

God is looking for a person, a church, and a city that will hear His gentle knock and open the door for Him. The Scriptures continually picture the Lord knocking on doors in both the Old and New Testaments. We see Him prophetically knocking on the door of His *own* house in the Song of Solomon, seeking the attention of His Beloved, the Church. (See Song of Solomon 5:2.)

Why would the door of His own house be locked? It is because He's given away the *key*. He told Peter the apostle, "I am giving you the key. Whatever you bind on earth is bound in heaven; whatever you loose on earth is loosed in heaven" (see Mt. 16:19). The Lord gave us the key to His own appearance when He *gave us the ability to open the windows of Heaven and close the gates of hell.* **The latch is on our side!** (But are the windows painted shut with man's traditions?) The Lover of our souls has persistently knocked at the doors of His House, but we respond exactly like Solomon's bride:

> *I have taken off my robe—must I put it on again? I have washed my feet—must I soil them again? (Song of Solomon 5:3 NIV)*

God's betrothed Lover and Bride has become too comfortable. She refuses to open the door because it isn't convenient. The cost of intimacy seems too high. The discomfort of it all has bred an apathy that urges us to move too slowly and casually when our Beloved knocks at our heart's door. Ominously, the *knocking stops*—in alarm we finally rouse ourselves like Solomon's lazy bride. When we finally run to the door to unlock it, all that is left is the fleeting fragrance of where He *used to be*.

> *I opened for my lover, but my lover had left; He was gone. My heart sank at His departure. I looked for Him but did not find Him. I called Him but He did not answer (Song of Solomon 5:6 NIV).*

This is the sad state of the overly contented Church today. We may find ourselves barren as David's wife Michal was. Could it be that David was never again intimate with her? The disgust she had for him locked the door to intimacy, joy, and fruitfulness. **The Church's reluctance to pay the seemingly high cost of intimate worship is the root cause of our barrenness.**

The Bride of Christ has grown accustomed to living in the King's house **in His absence**. If she would return to the passion and hunger of her first love, she would never be so content unless the King Himself were present with her in the house. Instead, the modern-day Church seems to stir just enough at the Master's knock to moan, "No, not now. Don't You see that I'm too comfortable to get up right know? Can't it wait? I have a headache. After all, I have already taken my shoes off and propped up my feet. Do I have to open the door for You right *now*?"

Tommy Tenney – *God's Favorite House*

What Do We Do?

A ren't you tired of trying to pass out tracts, knock on doors, and make things happen? We've been trying to make things happen for a long time. Now *He* wants to make it happen! Why don't you find out what He's doing and join in? That's what Jesus did. He said, "Father, what are You doing? That's what I'll do." (See John 5:19-20.)

God wants to move in with your church family. How long has it been since you've been so hungry for God that it consumed you to the point where you couldn't care less what people thought of you? I challenge you right now to forget about every distraction, every opinion, but one. What are you feeling right now as you read about how God Himself invaded these churches? Are you squelching it? What is gripping your heart? Don't you feel the awakening of what you thought was a long-dead hunger? How long has it been since you felt what you're feeling right now? Rise up and pursue His presence. Become a God chaser.

I'm not talking about the excitement of praise and worship, as we would call it. We know how to get the music "just right" so the singing is stunning, the accompaniment is awesome, and everything seems perfect. But that's not what I'm talking about, and that's not what is causing your hunger right now. I'm talking about a hunger for *God's presence.* I said "a hunger for *God's presence.*"

Let me be blunt for a moment. I know in my heart of hearts that the truth of the matter is this: The Church has lived in self-righteous smugness for so long that we stink in God's nostrils. He can't even look at us in our present state. In the same way that you or I might feel embarrassed in a restaurant or grocery store when we see someone's children acting up and getting away with it, God feels the same way about our self-righteousness. God is uncomfortable with our smug self-righteousness. We are not "as together" as we think we are.

"What causes this kind of thing to happen?"

"Repentance."

In those days came John the Baptist, preaching in the wilderness of Judaea,

And saying, **Repent ye: for the kingdom of heaven is at hand.**

For this is he that was spoken of by the prophet Esaias, saying, The voice of one crying in the wilderness, **Prepare ye the way of the Lord, make His paths straight** (Matthew 3:1-3).

Repentance prepares the way and makes the road of our hearts straight. Repentance builds up every low place and takes down every high place in our lives and church families. *Repentance prepares us for His presence.* In fact, you cannot live in His presence without repentance. Repentance permits pursuit of His presence. It builds the road for you to get to God (or for God to get to you!). Just ask John the Baptist. When he built the road, Jesus "came walking."

This is the crux of what I have to say: How long has it been since you said, "I'm going for God"? How long has it been since you laid aside everything that ever occupied you and ran down the road of repentance to *pursue God?*

Tommy Tenney – *The God Chasers*

Exchange Your Weights for Power to Run the Race

*A*re there weights in your life—things you've taken upon yourself—that are not the burden of the Lord? He wants you to lay them aside in exchange for power to run the race! Unnecessary weights will weary your mind and turn you into a zombie in the spiritual world.

God's Word says you can take care of that by unloading or flinging off that weight. If it's a sin, repent of it. If it is a weight or care you have brought on yourself, lay it aside. Are you overloaded with the unrealistic expectations of others? Unload them before you become a slave in the "Kingdom of They-dom." The bottom line is that "the government is on His shoulder," not the shoulders of your critics or would-be slave drivers. (See Isaiah 9:6.) Please God before you please man.

Have you noticed that whenever you set out to do something for the Lord, it seems like the enemy paints a target on your shield? It is easy to get overloaded when this happens because if the enemy can't get to you by one means, he always tries another. If you feel worn down and short-circuited like a battery that has run dry, then try the power that comes with unloading! Set your priorities and let Him determine your load.

God made us with two ends—one to think with, the other to sit on. The end you use determines whether you win or lose: Heads you win, tails you lose! Trite as it may sound, if you are so overloaded and burdened with things not of God that you virtually "cannot move," then you will lose. Use your head. Learn the power of unloading and give your burdens to the Lord. Then we can accept the "burden of the Lord" and share the yoke with Jesus. He makes the burden easy to bear, and when He shares the burden, losers become winners every time! (See Matthew 11:29-30.)

Much of the excess "weight" we place on our souls comes from wrong thinking. This is one of the enemy's strongholds and negative thinking is his by-product. He wants you to be overburdened about things you cannot change. That is why the Bible instructs us to bring "every thought into captivity to the obedience of Christ" (2 Cor. 10:5b NKJV).

T.F. Tenney and Tommy Tenney – *Secret Sources of Power*

Mark the Memories That Stand Out About God

think back through your life in Christ and mark the memories of God's touch that stand out. Can you recall what the preacher preached the time you had your closest encounter with God? Can you remember what the singers sang? Few of us can recall those details, but all of us can distinctly remember what God's presence felt like at that encounter.

It's like an encounter with electricity. If you have ever been shocked, you never forget what it felt like. *If He has even come close...you never forget!* I long for those times. I live for those moments.

The principle is simple: The more smoke you make, the closer you can get. Again, *the key is worship.* The value of worship is not measured in terms of volume and intensity. We know more about praise than we know about worship. Thanksgiving gets you in the gates, praise gets you in the courts, but worship takes you into His presence. We often get stalled in the courtyard and never make it to the throne room. Perhaps the low bow required when we enter the throne room and first see the King is a bit too humbling for us. Repentance has never been popular with the flesh.

The Word of God tells us that there are *five distinct and definite things that open the windows of Heaven.* This isn't a formula; it is a lifestyle of worship and dedication to God first in all things. All of the following are various elements of worship.

1. *Tithing* is an ancient key to the heavenlies that even pre-dates the giving of the law to Abraham (see Gen. 14:18-20). The principle of giving God the "firstfruits" of our income or increase is clearly described in the Book of Malachi:

   > *"Bring all the tithes into the storehouse, that there may be food in My house, and try Me now in this," says the Lord of hosts, "If I will not **open for you the windows of heaven** and pour out for you such blessing that there will not be room enough to receive it"* (Malachi 3:10 NKJV).

2. *Persecution* also opens the heavens, as demonstrated in the Book of Acts when Stephen was martyred:

   > *But he, being full of the Holy Spirit, gazed into heav-en and saw the glory of God, and Jesus standing at the right hand of God, and said, "Look! **I see the heavens opened** and the Son of Man standing at the right hand of God!" Then they cried out with a loud voice...and they cast him out of the city and stoned him* (Acts 7:55-58a NKJV).

3. *Persistence* is an effective tool for "prying open" the gates of Heaven. Elijah prayed seven times and kept sending his ser-vant back to search the skies until, on the seventh time, the servant saw a cloud the size of a man's hand rise from the sea. That tiny cloud from God grew into such a powerful storm that the skies were turned black with rain and wind. (See 1 Kings 18:42-45.) Jesus told the disciples that the "door" would be opened to those who persistently ask, seek, and knock on God's door. (See Matthew 7:7-8.)

4. *Unity* will open the windows of Heaven; it invites God's pres-ence wherever two or three *agree* "concerning anything that they ask." Jesus literally said, "For where two or three are gathered together in My name, I am there in the midst of

them" (Mt. 18:19-20 NKJV). The opposite side of this principle is illustrated in Peter's warning to husbands and wives to remain united so their "prayers may not be hindered" (1 Pet. 3:7 NKJV).

5. *Worship* is the fifth key to the third heaven. David the psalmist prophesied, "Lift up your *heads*, O ye *gates*; and be ye lift up, ye *everlasting doors*; and the King of glory shall come in" (Ps. 24:7).Have you ever seen a "head" on a gate? It is obvious that David was referring to people as "gates" and "everlasting doors" through which the King of glory can come to the earth. This is a call to worship.

Like it or not, the only way we can begin to open the heavens over our churches and cities is to become giving, persistent, and unified worshipers who aren't afraid to sacrifice all for Christ.

Tommy Tenney – *God's Favorite House*

Empty Yourself, Be Filled With God's Power

t is said the average American speaks nine million words a year. Five million of those words are the words, *I, me, my,* or *mine.* It is a staggering statistic. It tells you something about the spirit of the age in which we live. It is a selfish age. All truth is parallel. God's solution for selfishness is death to self. Why should we be surprised when God calls for selfless leaders in a selfish age?

> *And whoever desires to be first among you, let him be your slave; just as the Son of Man did not come to be served, but to serve, and to give His life a ransom for many* (Matthew 20:27-28 NKJV).

Disciples are expected to live with a deeper level of relinquishment than new believers. In the same way, those who would lead and feed must relinquish more than they did as disciples.

Moses was fed at Pharaoh's table and he was subjected to the disciplines of the Egyptian royal house. He was educated and trained in all the ways of Egypt. This discipline took Moses to a high level of accomplishment in Egyptian society, but it counted for almost nothing in God's Kingdom. According to the Book of Acts, Moses was "learned in all the wisdom of the Egyptians, and was mighty in words and deeds" *until his 40th birthday* when he decided to visit his Hebrew brethren (see Acts 7:22-23 NKJV). He spent another 40 years in the desert of relinquishment before he was ready to do things God's way.

Moses was "mighty in speech" until he turned 40 and tried to fulfill his destiny on his own. Then he had an intimate encounter with God that apparently left him a stutterer! Sometimes what we consider to be "religious eloquence" is really a "spiritual stutter," an impediment to true communication with and for the Almighty.

Exaltation at one level is abasement at a higher. That is the power of relinquishment. We cannot pray, "Thy kingdom come..." unless first, we are willing to pray, "My kingdom go...." (See Matthew 6:10.) We have a tendency to hold onto "our kingdom" with a death grip, but we need to learn there is a power that comes through relinquishment.

God told His reluctant deliverer, Moses, "When I get through using you, the children of Israel are going to give Me glory. It will not be because of your education, your intelligence, or your ability to speak. *Your leadership ability will not get all the praise for what happens.*" Give man honor, but glory belongs to God alone.

God performed astounding miracles through Moses, yet as far as we know, God never healed him of his stutter. Sometimes God will leave a mark somewhere on your life as a permanent reminder of the time and place He touched you and changed you forever. It will be a place where He can always get a hold on you.

Moses could tell you about it, if you would be patient with his stuttering delivery. Jacob could tell you about his limp, but you would be able to see that for yourself. So it was with Paul's "thorn in the flesh." Regardless of the strength of his belief in the healing and delivering power of God, we have no record that Paul was healed or delivered of his thorn. It may have been God's means of getting Paul's attention. Paul put it this way:

> And **lest I should be exalted above measure through the abundance of the revelations**, *there was given to me a thorn in the flesh, the messenger of Satan to buffet me, lest I should be exalted above measure. For this thing I besought the Lord thrice, that it might depart from me. And He said unto me, My grace is sufficient for thee: for* **My [God's] strength is made perfect in weakness**. *Most gladly therefore will I rather glory in my infirmities, that the power of Christ may rest upon me (2 Corinthians 12:7-9 KJV).*

Moses was at the height of his career. He had power, prestige, wealth, and influence with the royal house of Pharaoh. However, he had a prior commitment and a divine commission from the royal house of the Most High God of Israel. He was called of God to deliver the children of Israel from their Egyptian bondage, but first he had to be freed of every shadow of his former house and changed from the heart outward. It took 40 years of shepherding in the wilderness to prepare him for the next 40 years in the place as a deliverer.

T.F. Tenney and Tommy Tenney – *Secret Sources of Power*

Feeling Drained?

*H*ave you ever felt powerless? My staff and I rely heavily on our cell phones. They can be a real lifesaver when you're on the road as much as we are. But cell batteries have only a limited life span; after a few hours of use, they need to be recharged.

One weary weekend, I was feeling just as drained as my cell phone battery. I checked in to the hotel and went through my evening routine, which included dutifully placing my cell phone in its "recharging cradle." Unfortunately, I neglected to plug the cradle into the wall! The next morning, I woke up refreshed—but my phone was no better than it had been the night before! My phone was in the right place, but it wasn't connected to the power source!

My embarrassing oversight prevented me from using my cell phone for a few hours that morning. That mistake was easily corrected...but sometimes the consequences of not "plugging in" can be much more severe. I wonder how many people dutifully march to church every week—maybe even several times each week—but leave just as drained as when they came? They're in the right place, but they're not plugged in to the power of God that is available to them!

It isn't enough to simply be in the right place. The fact that you occupy a pew in your church on a regular basis doesn't guarantee you a relationship with God—and without that relationship, it doesn't really matter if you sit in a pew or sit on a barstool. You can be the first person to arrive and the last to leave; you can study the Scriptures for hours on end, "ever learning, and never able to come to the knowledge of the truth" (2 Tim. 3:7); you can even do great things for God, but still lack power in your life. If I had left my cell phone on that unplugged charger for days or weeks instead of just overnight, it still wouldn't have helped. Multiplication of effort is not a substitute for true power!

Are you feeling drained? Do the activities that were once life-giving now seem empty and meaningless to you? Does your heart cry out because you know that there is more available than what you are currently tapping into? We know that our physical bodies require constant replenishment. If we fail to eat, drink, or sleep, we will suffer for it. Similarly, our spiritual bodies also need recharging.

I know what it is like to feel drained. Often, when I get that way, I'll spend some time with my Dad. You don't have to run a marathon to feel physically depleted, and you don't have to be a minister to experience spiritual weariness. My father has a way of recharging me even when he is feeling weary himself. He knows where the power source is. Through the years, he has learned how to remain connected to God and still connect with others. Man's use and abuse of power is chronicled in our history books, enshrined in our monuments, and glamorized in our legends. It is taught in our schools and promised in our pulpits. Commercials preach that certain products will empower us, or they threaten that lack of the same will leave us powerless. We have power lunches, power naps, and power bars—but even in this energized environment, true power often eludes us.

I've never met a "God chaser" who didn't occasionally grow weary in the chase. The only difference between a "God chaser" and a "pew warmer" is his/her determination to be plugged in. One secret to living a continuously empowered life is to guard yourself against the things that can disconnect you from the power source. Obviously, sin will do that—but so will weariness.

We cannot remain connected to God if we are weighted down by our busyness. We can spend so much time doing things for God that we neglect our relationship with Him. Good stewardship of our time isn't doing everything that we possibly can; it is doing everything that God wants us to do—no more, no less. We cannot be in His will if we have no time to pray and rest in His presence!

Bitterness and unforgiveness are also power drains; they steal our energy—physically, emotionally, and spiritually. Failure to forgive also can disconnect us from the power source. We cannot be fully committed to furthering God's Kingdom while we have set up and are still defending the borders of our personal kingdoms. The way up is down; to lay hold you must let go; to be filled you must become empty. It isn't the easy way...but if you want a power that doesn't rise and fall with circumstance and whim, it is the only way!

GodChasers.network Newsletter

The "Suddenly of God" Requires the "Waiting of Man"

"**S**uddenly" there came an upper room experience where He threw open the windows of Heaven and rushed down. That's what we want: the rushing in of God, that suddenly of God. *But you don't have the "suddenly of God" without the "waiting of man."* We need to go after the face of God. We can no longer be content with God's just slipping His hand out from under the veil to dispense gospel goodies to us anymore. We want the veil to open, and we want to pass through into the Holy of Holies to have a life-changing encounter with Him. Then we need to prop open that veil with Davidic passion and worship so the glory of God will manifest itself in the streets of the city.

The Church is pregnant with God's purposes. Our body feels swollen; our belly is distended. We don't know when or where the baby will be born, but we know a baby is about to be born, and we are desperate. To be honest, I hope you live with so much holy frustration that you can't sleep tonight. I pray that a gnawing hunger for the presence of God rises up in your heart with devastating results. I want you to be "ruined" for everything except His purposes.

On the day the Church rises up to build a mercy seat according to the pattern of Heaven, God will wave good-bye to Michael and Gabriel and will literally set up a throne zone in our midst! Let me assure you that when the glory of God shows up like that, we won't have to advertise or promote anything. Once the Bread of Heaven takes His seat among us, the hungry will come.

"Father, we fan the flames of hunger.

May we never be the same. Set our hearts on fire."

There is only one way you and I can pay the price of obedience to create a throne zone on earth. We need to let our hearts be so broken before Him that the things that break His heart also break our hearts.

Put your hand on your heart and, if you dare, pray this prayer:

"Break my heart, Lord;

I don't want to be the same.

Soften my heart, Lord Jesus,

and let me dwell in Your presence."

People don't understand what it means to be caught in an outbreak of the manifest presence of God. Duncan Campbell described an incident in the Hebrides that was burned into his memory.

"At my request several officers from the parish visited the island, bringing with them a young lad who recently was brought to the saving knowledge. After spending time and prayer at the cottage, we went to the church to find it crowded now. But seldom did I experience such bondage of spirit, and preaching was most difficult, so much so that when only half way through my address I stopped preaching.

"Just then my eye caught sight of this young lad who was visibly moved, and appeared to be deeply burdened. Leaning over the pulpit I said, 'Donald, will you lead us in prayer.' There was an immediate response, and in that moment the flood gates of heaven opened, and the congregation was struck as by a hurricane, and many cried out for mercy.

"But the most remarkable feature of this visitation was not what happened there in the church, but the spiritual impact on the island. Men, who until that moment had no thought of seeking after God, were suddenly arrested where they stood, sat or laid, and became deeply concerned about their soul, until they said, This is the Lord's doing" (Duncan Campbell, from conversations with Alan Vincent.)

Tommy Tenney – *God's Favorite House*

I Plead the Blood!

Some of the old-timers from the early days of the Pentecostal outpouring used to frequently say, "I plead the blood! I plead the blood of Jesus!" This powerful phrase needs to be restored to our vocabulary because there is still power in that blood.

Several years ago a man and his wife were in a very serious car accident. When the man came to himself, he realized his wife was bleeding profusely next to him. As people started to rush to the car to see if they could help, he reached over and laid his hand on his wife who was literally bleeding to death. People who were strangers to God's way walked up and heard him saying, "I plead the blood. I plead the blood. I plead the blood."

This man testifies today that Jesus' blood flow stopped his wife's blood flow! The people who gathered around the couple that day didn't understand what was happening, but the angels of God and the Almighty Himself certainly understood his language. Their lives were spared because there is healing and delivering power in the blood!

The same man served as Foreign Missions Director of his denomination in the late '60s and '70s. Frequently his travels took him to Asia and Africa, and he noticed that on occasion, the strange demons from a foreign country would follow him home! He said, "I had fought them all night long, and there were some strange ones. In the middle of the night they would wake me up. I would hear my children wake up crying because of a spiritual attack of fear, and not knowing why they were afraid. They didn't know, but I did. Not that I was a spiritual giant, I just would know exactly what it was."

He said he would get up and go through his house from room to room, being careful not to skip "one nook or cranny"—and plead the blood of Jesus: "I plead the blood! I plead the blood!" He commanded in the name of Jesus and by the power of the blood that every evil spirit return from whence it came. The peace of God would always flood the house as the enemy forces had to make their exit. The man was T.F. Tenney.

The blood protects—the blood purges—the blood is victorious. The events of the first Passover proved that even the Death Angel has to back up when he sees the power of the blood of the Lamb.

Did you know the blood talks? According to the writer of Hebrews, "The blood of sprinkling [the blood of Jesus]...speaks better things than that of Abel" (Heb. 12:24b NKJV). According to the Bible, the "blood" we are talking about is *the blood of God.* (See Acts 20:28.) In other words, *the only blood God ever had flowed through the veins of Jesus Christ.* The power of the blood sealed Christ's victory at Calvary.

An agnostic would have us believe that if Jesus is truly God and if Jesus died, then God died at Calvary. The objection is simple: *All of God that could die, died at Calvary.* We are speaking of the flesh of the Lamb slain before the foundation of the earth.

We must have vital faith in the precious blood of Jesus. It is not enough to simply repeat the rhetoric or say the words, "I plead the blood." It is believing something happens when you say it. "I plead the blood of Jesus! It talks for me! It will slap the devil right in the face for me."

When the enemy extends his clammy hand toward some area of your life, a voice you didn't hear booms into satan's darkness just as he is ready to close his grip. "Get your hands off My child!" Immediately the devil's grip loosens. He says to himself, "Oh no! I recognize that voice. It is the voice of the blood of the Lamb. I cannot do this. I can stay out here and howl and froth and lie and try to frighten this man, but I cannot lay my hand on him. It's not fair. He is under the blood and I cannot go there."

For 15 centuries, Israel had a sanctuary containing a special area called the Holy of Holies. It would mean death to anyone, except the priest, who entered that place. It had one message and it was simple: Man cannot dwell in the presence of Almighty God.

T.F. Tenney and Tommy Tenney – *Secret Sources of Power*

We Must Be Proficient at One Level Before Moving to the Next

Good possesses all wisdom, and He requires us to become proficient at one level of obedience and faith before He moves us up to the next level. We can be confident in God's thoughts toward us. He said, "For I know the thoughts that I think toward you, says the Lord, thoughts of peace and not of evil, to give you a future and a hope" (Jer. 29:11 NKJV). Best of all, Jesus promised He would never leave us or forsake us. (See Hebrews 13:5b.)

Satan's real war is with God; we are not the primary target in his schemes. He assaults the people and purposes of God in the earth because he is powerless to hurt God. He has to settle for hurting God by hurting His people and by provoking them to disappoint God through disobedience or apathy. The devil is simply obsessed with the desire to insult the Bride of Christ.

Another aspect of satan is that he is a counterfeiter to the core. Paul spoke of "the mystery of Christ," referring to God's plan through Christ to reconcile to Himself *people of all races, tribes, and nations,* whether they were physically descended from Abraham or not. (See Ephesians 3:3-4.) Satan the counterfeiter responded with "the mystery of iniquity (or lawlessness)," which is simply the construction of a *false church* built with "power, signs, and lying wonders" alongside the true Church of God. This is the best the author of confusion could do. (See 2 Thessalonians 2:7-9.)

Satan's religious "church" of fallacy claims God's name but lives in sin, loves the world, and denies that God or His people have any real spiritual power. (See 2 Timothy 3:1-9.) The adversary may manage to fool a large percentage of people most of the time, but God knows those who are His own.

Don't sell the dominion Jesus restored to you on the cross. Everything that was lost due to Adam's sin in the beginning is available to us in Jesus Christ, the "second Adam" and the Lord of glory. The Bible says, "The kingdoms of this world have become the kingdoms of our Lord and of His Christ..." (Rev. 11:15b NKJV). The knowledge of the glory of God is going to cover the earth as the waters cover the sea. (See Habakkuk 2:14.) What a day that will be!

Satan is presently the prince and power of the air; the Bible says he is lord/god of this world. He is also Beelzebub, lord of the flies. And think of the places where flies flock—places of rottenness and refuse. Finally, he's cast into a bottomless pit. His kingdom is in "free fall"— diminishing power, while Christ's Kingdom is ascending. Don't buy stock in the wrong kingdom!

The devil is still operating as the prince of the power of the air. In the eyes of the unredeemed world, he may still serve as their god of pleasure and self-gratification. However, his time is short and his power limited. God has given the Church authority over the "power behind the throne" in this world. This is yet another secret source of power to every child of the light and disciple of the King of kings and Lord of lords.

T.F. Tenney and Tommy Tenney – *Secret Sources of Power*

God Felt Strongly About David's Pursuit of His Presence

Somehow David captured something of the essence of God, something that no one else seemed to accomplish. I don't understand how this all works, but I do know that *David's passion for God's presence is crucial—I just hope it's contagious*. Recently I've heard the hint from Heaven: **"If you build it, I will come."**

Remember that David is the only man described in the Scriptures in this way: "I have found David the son of Jesse, *a man after Mine own heart*, which shall fulfil all My will" (Acts 13:22b). I am convinced that there are two meanings to the phrase, "after Mine own heart." The standard interpretation is that David was a man who was "like" God's heart or "whose heart was like" God's heart.

I also believe that David was a man who was constantly *"after"* God's heart. *He was a God chaser, a pursuer of God's manifest presence*. His determination to bring the ark to Jerusalem is living proof of his passion for the Presence. This second interpretation is supported by David's unmatched descriptions of his intimate spiritual walk with God in the Psalms.

I won't go into all the details, but there are many similarities between the tabernacle of David, the temple Solomon built, and the tabernacle of Moses. The tabernacle of Moses and Solomon's temple featured three distinct enclosed areas: the outer court, the Holy

Place, and the Holy of Holies. A great veil (a heavy drapery in our modern colloquialism) was stretched across the tabernacle to separate the Holy Place from the Holy of Holies where the ark of the covenant rested.

The ark was a gold-covered wooden box originally built by Moses according to instructions he received from God. Its lid was fitted with solid gold figures of cherubim (two angelic figures) facing each other with outstretched wings. The space between them was called "the mercy seat," and this is where the blue flame of God's manifest presence hovered (also *shekinah* glory). The ark, the mercy seat, and the blue flame of God's presence were always hidden behind the thick fabric of the veil.

God never did like that veil. He had to have it, but He didn't like it. When Jesus died on the cross at Calvary, God was the one who ripped the veil from top to bottom in the temple of Herod in Jerusalem. He ripped it in such a way that it could never be rewoven again. *He hated that veil like a prisoner hates his cell door!* It represented the wall, the dividing line that separated Him from mankind. Until that day on Calvary, God had to hide behind the veil to preserve the life of the fallen humanity that came to worship Him in His holiness.

Tommy Tenney – *God's Favorite House*

Keepers Weepers, Losers Finders

Children at play like to say, "Finders keepers, losers weepers!" Jesus said, "Whoever loses his life will find it." The law of His Kingdom is "keepers weepers, losers finders." The power of relinquishment is released when you pray, "Father, I give You my self, my reputation, my education, my past, my future, and my present. I want the very best You have for me."

You must keep praying until you reduce all your desires into one—to serve the Lord with all your heart, soul, and might. Pray until all your fear is reduced to one fear—the fear of the Lord. In that moment you will experience a glorious liberty. As for the "rod in your hand," the ordinary tools of service God put in your life, they will be transformed into the "rod of God."

Moses' rod was once a simple shepherd's crook, a tool for herding sheep and steadying the shepherd's step in places of uncertain footing. When Moses learned to fear God more than man and laid down his rod at God's command, the Lord took ownership of Moses' rod and used it to miraculously deliver the children of Israel from their bondage. God seeks ordinary people who will simply relinquish themselves to Him. It is truly amazing what God will do when we make ourselves genuinely available to Him.

Two of the ordinary people used by God in the Old Testament participated in one of the strangest battles ever fought in the history of man. When the men of Amalek decided to pick a fight with Moses and the Israelites, Moses told a man named Joshua to pick out some men and "go fight with Amalek tomorrow." The only reassurance he gave Joshua was this: "Tomorrow I will stand on the top of the hill with the rod of God in my hand" (Ex. 17:9b NKJV). Joshua's chief credential was that he served Moses faithfully as his assistant.

Meanwhile, a second ordinary man named Hur climbed a hill with Moses and Aaron the high priest. As long as Moses held up the rod of God in his hand, then Joshua and the Israelites won. When the rod went down the Amalekites prevailed.

Joshua could have looked up from the battlefield and said, "Moses, why don't *you* come down here and fight?" but he didn't. Had he done it, Moses would have said, "I *am* fighting here. It is just a different kind of fight."

T.F. Tenney and Tommy Tenney – *Secret Sources of Power*

Just Tell Me— Is That Him?

As Jesus passed through the gate, the blind beggar on the side of the road turned to someone standing nearby and asked a question:

"Is that Him? Just tell me, is that Him?"

"Yeah, yeah, Bartimaeus; that's Him."

"Then you better get out of my way because I'm about to lose my dignity."

Hear me, friend. *You can't preserve your dignity and seek His Deity. You can't save your face and seek His face.* At some point you are going to have to lose your spiritual manners. You will have to leave your Pentecostal, Baptist, or Presbyterian protocol behind you. You need to forget what you are supposed to do when, where, and how. You will have to reduce it down to the basics: "Is that Him? I think He's in the building! I think He's close." I don't know how you feel, but I refuse to let Him get that close to me and pass me by. "Jesus, Son of David, have mercy on me!"

Would Jesus pass us by? Absolutely. Jesus would have passed by the disciples when they were rowing a boat across the Sea of Galilee in the darkness of the night, but *they cried out to Him.* (See John 6:16-21.) He would have walked past the blind man, but Bartimaeus called out and kept calling out until Jesus turned aside to see him. Jesus would have walked past the woman with the incurable bleeding problem too, but she stretched out her hand and touched the hem of His garment by faith. (See Mark 5:25-34.) In the end, Jesus walked through Jerusalem countless times over the course of His brief life on earth, but the religious people of that ancient city missed the moment and the hour of their visitation.

One of the keys to turning visitation of the Spirit into habitation of the Spirit is recognizing Him. Has it been so long since you've "seen" Him? Would you recognize Him if He comes on a colt instead of a stallion? Would you embrace His visitation in humility as much as in power?

Would you believe me if I told you that Someone is knocking at the door of the Church right now? He is literally knocking at the door of His own house because He has given us the key. I don't want to see the Church miss her moment or hour of visitation. If somebody would ever open the door to Him, we won't be left to talk sadly about what He smelled like "the last time He knocked at our door." We will be walking with Him and fellowshiping with Him. Perhaps you sense something gripping your heart that makes you want to shout, "Lord, don't pass me by! Jesus, have mercy!"

"Father, I pray right now for a spirit of Bartimaeus to grip Your people. May we lay aside the garments of pride that identify us with the blind and lift our voices in worship, 'Jesus, Son of David!' We lift our voices in repentance, 'Have mercy on us.' We worship and repent and cry out, 'Don't pass us by!' "

Why don't you forget about your manners right now? It is time to lay aside your religious protocols, the things that dictate what is supposed to happen and when. *God has always preferred spiritual hunger over spiritual ritual.* Are you going to miss your moment? If you can feel Him edging closer and closer, then don't let Him get this close and pass you by, even while reading this book. Remember that *God is shopping for a place to break out.* He is knocking at the door. I can almost hear Him say to us, *"You know what happens when I visit a church.* **You've not yet seen what happens when I visit a city. Open the door and let Me in!"**

Tommy Tenney – *God's Favorite House*

So Close...
but So Far Away

I remember many years (and many pounds!) ago, I used to run track in school. At times it was a gargantuan effort to put one foot in front of another...pains in my side, breath coming in short gasps...only to hear the coach yell, "You're almost there—don't quit now!"

I was reminded of that while I was on a missions trip to Europe. (About 20 percent of my available ministry time is spent overseas.) This was a very special trip: My wife and three daughters were with me. On this particular afternoon we were spending some "daddy time" together. My then seven-year-old daughter, Andrea, had seen *The Hunchback of Notre Dame* and had begged us to take her to see Notre Dame Cathedral itself.

I took a wrong turn getting off of the Paris subway, and instead of walking down the street where Notre Dame was, we wound up walking along a street that ran parallel to it and turning the opposite direction. In the excitement of the moment and the enjoyment of just being together, I didn't realize my error. I knew that I was in the general area, but there were no signs to back up my belief. Andrea began to get tired. "It won't be too much further now," we encouraged her. But weary seven-year-old feet can only endure so much encouragement. In a flurry of drama that rivaled even the best stage performances, an exhausted Andrea threw herself down on a park bench and declared, "Daddy don't know where he's going!" She had reached her limit, and she wasn't going to take another step.

The truth was, I didn't know where I was going. But when we looked up from the place where she had stopped, we could see Notre Dame. We were just a few hundred feet from our goal! For awhile it seemed as though no amount of coaxing would persuade her to leave that bench...but, finally, we completed the journey together and toured the grandeur of Notre Dame Cathedral.

We're often like that. We'll start off in hot pursuit, full of energy and expectation, enthusiastic for the journey, barely able to contain ourselves. We imagine what it will be like when we reach our goal. Perhaps we even start running...hoping that by hastening our steps, we'll arrive even earlier. We're not really sure exactly where we're going and we don't know how much further we have to go, but around every corner lies the tantalizing hope that perhaps we've almost made it.

Enthusiasm won't keep us going for long, though. Aching feet and tired bodies overpower hope and weary spirits and exhausted minds disable faith as corner after corner yields no sign that we're any closer than when we began. Reality sets in, and the joy of the journey evaporates like a morning mist. The temptation is to just give up—to conclude that we'll never reach the goal, or that we've been going the wrong way the whole time.

Perhaps you've been there. Maybe you're reading this devotional exhausted and sprawled out on a park bench of your own—dejected and determined that you will *not* take *one more* step. You thought that your Father knew where He was taking you, but obviously this isn't where you wanted to be. You could be sulking in the very shadow of your desired destination! So close...yet so far away!

You are in good company. After Jesus' resurrection but before Pentecost, Jesus told the disciples to linger in Jerusalem until they were clothed in power from on high. (See Acts 1:4.) We're not explicitly told in Scripture how many people heard that command, but Paul tells us in First Corinthians 15 that Jesus appeared to more than 500 people after His resurrection. That even seems to be a small number compared to the thousands of lives Jesus touched during His earthly ministry. Yet in the Book of Acts, we're told that by the Day of Pentecost there were only 120 believers.

What happened to everyone else? Where did they go? How could so many who had gotten so close to Jesus Himself just walk away?

I wonder how many would-be disciples left the Upper Room the day before the Day of Pentecost. It must have been discouraging as night after night passed and the promise didn't materialize. They weren't told how long to wait...just to wait until. What a frustrating directive—to wait for an undetermined period of time for an unknown sign. How would you have felt if you had left the Upper Room the day before the Day of Pentecost?

Being a "God chaser" isn't easy. It takes more than just enthusiasm and good intentions to "catch" Him. It also takes perseverance. There will be times when we'll want to quit—when the road ahead of us seems so long and so difficult that we don't believe we'll ever make it. Those are the times when God can develop our character. Gifts can be given, but character must be developed. We enjoy receiving the gifts...but we don't enjoy our transit times in the "wilderness."

GodChasers.network newsletter

No More Stumbling in the Dark

*H*ow do you turn on the light of the glory of God? If you were raised in an older house or if you ever visited Grandma's house where the old-fashioned light fixtures had pull strings hanging from the ceiling, you will understand what I am about to say.

Do you remember what it was like trying to find that little pull string in the dark? There were no wall switches conveniently located beside the door. If you wanted to turn on the light in the middle of the night, there was only one way to do it. You had to "wade into the darkness" blindly waving your hands in the general direction of the pull string. Perhaps you have even barked your shin or stubbed your toe on furniture while stumbling around in the dark trying to find that string.

If we could somehow capture on videotape some of the crazy things people do when they are trying to find pull-string light switches, it would be hilarious. People on the hunt for pull-string light switches often wave their arms like madmen. They jump in desperation; they crouch down, halfway expecting a painful meeting with the shin-cracking edge of the coffee table. The more cautious ones reach up with one hand over their head and wave it back and forth....

The same thing happens in our churches sometimes. People who come in for the first time and see us going through some odd antics in our services ask, "What in the world are you doing?" All we can tell them is, *"We're hunting for the light switch.* If we can ever turn on the light of the glory of God in this place, you will under-stand." We may stumble around and wave our arms aimlessly for a time while we search for the light switch, but we know that the pre-existent light of God's glory means everything! If we can just turn on the light of His glory, then suddenly everyone will see and know the difference between truth and error. Most people will choose truth when given the opportunity; it is just that *they have never have had enough light around them to see the way.* The light of God's glory existed before the sun and moon, and it will continue to exist after they have been snuffed out. Somehow it must be made manifest!

Once we find out how to turn on the light of God's glory, we can determine how to *keep* that spiritual light shining. *This is what I call an open heaven!* We must keep the heavens open over that place of easy access to God's presence. When you live under an open heav-en, the same altar call that used to bring two people to the Lord will inexplicably bring 200 running forward to receive Christ. That is comparable to the difference between sawing lumber with a hand-saw and doing the same job with a power saw. For generations, we have struggled to free the lost from satan's bondage using the anointing. God has opened the door for us to do it much quicker and easier through the revelation of *His glory* in our lives and churches. The anointing can quickly draw a crowd, and it can easily affect a crowd. However, when God comes down and reveals His glory among us, the entire city will be affected!

The ministry of Charles G. Finney was marked by city-transform-ing revivals. The city of Utica, New York, was dramatically changed by the power of God resident in the life of Finney, a man who burned with the passion of deep prayer and an intimate relationship with God.

It is said that when Finney walked through the knitting mills of Utica in the late 1800's, the presence of God was so strong that workers began to fall to their knees in repentance even before he opened his mouth! Ultimately, the entire city and region were affect-ed because of the presence of God he carried with him. *It was as if he carried a light with him that suddenly allowed men to view them-selves and God from a right perspective.* When the Presence came near, men knew that they were dirty and that God was holy! This seems to be a modern-day fulfillment of Isaiah's prophecy:

> *Arise, shine; for your light has come! And the glory of the Lord is risen upon you. For behold, the darkness shall cover the earth, and deep darkness the people; but the Lord will arise over you, and His glory will be seen upon you. The Gentiles shall come to your light, and kings to the brightness of your rising* (Isaiah 60:1-3 NKJV).

While ministering in that city, I asked my host to take me to the same mills Finney visited so many years before. The mills were abandoned long ago, and the people who worked there and experienced the power of God are gone now. Even so, the potential of God still seems to linger in the silence of those buildings. I leaned against the wall of one of the mills and just wept as I prayed, "God, I want to be a person who props open the windows of Heaven so much that people will have an encounter with You just by being around me."

Tommy Tenney – *God's Favorite House*

In the Right Place

A young man who interviewed six elderly prayer veterans of the New Hebrides revival said, "One of them looked at me with fire in his ancient eyes, and he said in a broken brogue, '*If you ever find Him, never, never, never, never let go!*'" The experiences and insights that these men shared with their young interviewer were recorded for posterity on an audiotape that I have in my possession. I just can't get over those words, "If you ever find Him, never, never, never, never let go!"

What do these words mean? They mean that if you manage to get the door of Heaven propped open, don't ever let it close again. You might be left at a useless door of the past, guarding only the fragrance of what used to be. Now you will find yourself running through the streets like the bride of Solomon, desperately asking other people, "Have you see Him? His head and hair are white like wool. I didn't know it was Him; I was too tired when He knocked."

Desperate God chasers are being graced to "catch Him" in divine visitation more than ever, and there is heavenly purpose in it all. Every day I hear more reports of people stumbling on their knees through doors or gates in time that let them peek into eternity. The same thing happened to Jacob when he went to sleep too close to a gate between the heavens. He awoke with a clear vision of an open Heaven before him, and it marked the beginning of a permanent change in his life.

When we find ourselves in places of divine visitation, it is like a seam in time has opened up before us. When Eternity Himself enters our little playhouse in the land of time, everything of earthly importance seems to fade away. Why? *Because God is in the house.* Eternity has visited our little time-bound world, and His glory is filling up our cramped room. That is why three hours seem like a mere three minutes when we get lost in His presence in the midst of our worship. In those moments, we have come closest to the gate. We can almost slip the surly bonds of time into the timeless realm of eternity.

When Jacob stumbled across the gate of Heaven, he set up stones to mark the place and said, "I don't want to forget this." However, if we are not careful, we can use markers from this realm that don't fit the markers in the spirit realm.

Most people try to mark the "location" of their spiritual experiences with temporal, ever-changing markers. They may tell the worship leader, "Let's sing that song we sang three weeks ago, because we were singing it when I had a visitation of God." *Unfortunately, temporal markers can never mark a place of eternity.* That's why they come back to the worship leader and say, "Well, it's good, but it's not the same." The problem is they set up the wrong kind of marker. *They should have marked the position and hunger of their hearts, not the song.*

One time my grandfather took me to his favorite fishing spot. After he had carefully maneuvered the boat into just the right spot, he said, "Now, son, if you'll always fish at this little spot right here, you'll catch a lot of fish. Right here you are over a submerged outcropping."

I went back there later on and positioned my boat in the same area, but I didn't catch anything. When I got home, I called my grandfather and said, "Big Daddy, there weren't any fish there."

He said, "No, son, there's always fish there. You just weren't right on it."

"Well, I couldn't have been very far...."

"You don't understand, son," he said. "You don't have to be 50 feet away to miss the spot. You could be just two feet away from the right spot and still not catch any fish. You have to be right over it. Come on, I'll go with you this time."

We went back to Big Daddy's fishing spot once more and he said, "Now, you drive the boat and get it positioned." So I maneuvered the boat until I had it right where I thought it was supposed to be, and then I looked over at Big Daddy. He just smiled and said, "Son, you're not at the right spot—*it's over there.*"

Tommy Tenney – *God's Favorite House*

Up Is Down and You Die to Live

*J*esus said, "If anyone desires to be first, he shall be last of all and servant of all" (Mk. 9:35b NKJV). In God's economy, up is down and the way you live is to die. The way you get is to give because the laws of the Kingdom are reversed from the laws of this world. According to the law, in the shadow of Egypt you must grab and climb, regardless of who you step on. That just won't work if you import it into the church setting—you have to turn it loose.

God expects us to do some things for ourselves, but sometimes we get out of control and try to do everything ourselves. We must replace our stubborn compulsion to do our own thing with a willingness to "let go." Sin began because the devil said, "I will." Redemption was birthed because Jesus said, "Not My will, but Yours, be done" (Lk. 22:42b NKJV).

Paul knew how to relinquish things to God. He said, "And I will very gladly spend and be spent for your souls; though the more abundantly I love you, the less I am loved" (2 Cor. 12:15 NKJV). Paul wasn't offering a little here and a little there, a little now and a little later. He was offering everything unreservedly.

We don't mind the part about "spending and being willing to spend." We just have problems when we become the "currency" and the "being spent" part starts. Relinquishment comes into play when God starts taking things out of you and taking them away from you. Paul, for instance, had to learn how to love without being loved back. None of us like that part.

Moses was scrambling for excuses to avoid God's call when the Lord told him, "Okay, now put your hand in your bosom...now pull it out." Moses was shocked to see that his hand was covered with leprosy! What did he do to deserve that? Perhaps God wanted Moses to know that He knew there had been a little sin on those hands. "Put it back, now out again." When Moses withdrew his hand again, his skin was perfectly clean and clear again.

God was teaching Moses two lessons. First, any person who cannot control the flesh, cannot cast out the devil. You must know what is in your heart and keep your flesh clean through repentance and obedience. Then you can handle the devil.

Moses, put your hand on your heart. It will reveal what is hidden in your hands. The second lesson was that God cannot do miracles through anyone who wants control. God let Moses know who was in charge and where the power came from.

God intended to embarrass the devil and humble Pharaoh, but first He had to work on Moses' attitude. You will never be a success for the Kingdom until you see yourself as a threat to the enemy. We are more of a threat to him than he can be to us—when we relinquish ourselves to God.

You can be sure the process of relinquishment and preparation in life can get confusing at times. Moses tried to lead the children of Israel out of Egypt but things suddenly took a turn toward disaster. He and the Israelites ended up at the shore of the Red Sea with Pharaoh's army hot on their heels. Pharaoh had just come from the deathbed of his firstborn and there was vengeance in his eyes and violence in his heart. His pursuit of the Jewish people was relentless, and Moses knew he was coming.

The people said, "We ought to go *back* to Egypt."

Moses said, "*Stand still.*"

God said, "*Go forward.*"

Sometimes we find ourselves in a similar place. People around us ask, "What are you doing moving in *that* direction? Go back to where you were comfortable." Meanwhile, a leader you respect may say, "Maybe you ought to just stay put for awhile. Maybe the timing is just not right." The only way to find your way among conflicting opinions is to ask this question: What does *God* say? "Go forward."

T.F. Tenney and Tommy Tenney – *Secret Sources of Power*

The Power of the Blood Goes Beyond Sin

he writer of Hebrews declared, "...according to the law almost all things are purified with blood, and without shedding of blood there is no remission" (Heb. 9:22 NKJV). Notice the passage does not say "remission of *sin.*" Sin is definitely included, but the power of the blood does not end when it takes care of sin. It purges *almost* everything. Without the shedding of blood there is no remission.

Priests in the Old Testament sprinkled almost everything with blood. What wasn't sprinkled with blood was dabbed with anointing oil. They had complete confidence in the power of the blood to cleanse, deliver, protect. *It was a total purgative.* It was the key to remission and pardon and liberty.

Luke often used the word *remission* in his Gospel or record of the Good News. According to his report, Jesus Himself implied that it was to be part of what we call "the apostle's doctrine" when He said, "...repentance and remission of sins should be preached in His name to all nations... (Lk. 24:47 NKJV).

Luke was a physician, and the medical concept of "remission" meant then what it means now. If someone with a malignancy or disease in their body experiences a significant improvement in their condition, they are said to be "in remission." It means the disease process has been arrested or is in retreat.

The blood of the Lamb attacks sin and chases it away. Sin retreats in the presence of the washing of the blood of Jesus. The works of the flesh go in remission when the power of the blood drives them out. There is good reason for the enemy to fear the blood. Even sin recognizes the blood. The demons of hell quake and tremble at the mention of the blood of the Lamb.

We must learn the principles that lead to the release of the power of the blood in our lives. We face days of unparalleled destiny for the Church in the midst of unparalleled darkness. We need to recognize the efficacy, or the force and power of the blood in our day and time.

The Lord said to the Israelites, "For *the life of the flesh is in the blood*, and I have given it to you upon the altar to make atonement for your souls; for *it is the blood that makes atonement for the soul*" (Lev. 17:11 NKJV). The word *atonement* means "covering."

The blood of the Lamb does more than simply deliver us from sin; its power covers and protects. Even more than that, it is a tool and a weapon we can use to deliver, cover, and protect others.

When God told Moses about the "dividing line" or "division" He would put around the Israelites in Egypt, He used a very specific word that is important to our understanding of the power of the blood. He said, "And I will put a *division* between My people and thy people" (Ex. 8:23a KJV). (The *New King James Version* says, "I will make a *difference*....") The Hebrew of that passage reads, "I will put *redemption* between My people and thy people." The power of the blood preempts and protects us from the plagues of the devil.

T.F. Tenney and Tommy Tenney – *Secret Sources of Power*

If I Can Just Get My Hands in That Crack

W here are the doorkeepers? God knows we need doorkeepers more than we need kings and presidents. We need people who know how to access His presence and open the door for the glory of God to come into our homes, churches, cities, and nations. David again writes the vision so we can run:

> Lift up your heads, O you **gates**! And be lifted up, **you everlasting doors**! And the King of glory shall come in (Psalm 24:7 NKJV).

Gates don't have heads. It is obvious that *we* are the gates in this Psalm. If we lift up our heads, what happens? The Hebrew literalization of that phrase is "be *opened* up you everlasting doors." When we obey this command, the King of glory Himself will come in. What does all this mean? We, as the Church, are literally the gateway for the rest of the world to have an encounter with God. *When you stand in the place of worship, you are literally opening up and swinging wide a spiritual gate, an entrance for the risen Lord.* A modern-day David named Martin Smith sings a new song based on an ancient theme:

> "Fling wide your heavenly gates.
>
> Prepare the way of the risen Lord..."

This call to worship must be the anthem of the Church.

We are called to take our place beside our great High Priest and stand in the gap between the world who doesn't know and those who do. We are holding open the rapidly closing "elevator" that takes people to Heaven. Sometimes I can sense a crack in the heavenlies even as I preach messages to congregations in certain places, where it seems like the heavens are about to open. I sometimes think to myself, *If I can just get my hands in that crack and **pry** it or **pray** it open, maybe the glory of God will come down tonight.*

Gatekeepers are rare and priceless in God's economy. Perhaps David peered into the darkness of the night one evening and felt reassured when he saw the dancing feet and outstretched arms of the late-shift worship team filtering the glory of God and was inspired to write,

Behold, bless the Lord, all you servants of the Lord, who by night stand in the house of the Lord! Lift up your hands in the sanctuary, and bless the Lor (Psalm 134:1-2 NKJV).

If we ever want to move from a visitation of God to a habitation of God, someone has to learn how to hold open the door to the heavenlies. It appears that some of us would prefer to go inside the veil and let the door swing shut behind us. We don't care about the world as long as we get in. I'm sorry, maybe it is because of the Southern culture in which I was raised, but I was taught to be a gentleman. You don't just walk through a door and let it shut behind you. You hold it open for others. I think it is time for the Church to pick up some spiritual etiquette and say, "Let's hold open the door of Heaven." Then those who watch us from afar can say, "Bless the Lord, all you servants of the Lord, who by night stand in the house of the Lord"—*propping open the heavens.*

How long have you been praying for an open heaven over your church and community? I promise you it is *not nearly as long as He has been waiting behind the door for it to open.* In the Song of Solomon, we see Him pictured as the loving groom, peering through the latticework for some glimpse of His beloved. He is waiting behind the door saying, "If I can ever get My Church into position, then I can throw open the windows and gates of Heaven and pour out...."

Tommy Tenney – God's Favorite House

We Dance at the Veil and Refuse to Go In

The Word of God tells us that the veil of division was torn in two by Jesus Christ's death on Calvary, and that we have free entry into God's presence through the blood of Jesus. We just aren't entering in. Occasionally somebody falls or stumbles his way past the veil during our dancing sessions and then comes back with a wild-eyed stare. But we usually go back into our dancing mode right in front of the veil. We get all excited about the possibility but we never really consummate the process. *The purpose of the anointing is to help us make the transition from flesh into glory.* One reason we like to linger in the anointing is that it makes the flesh feel good. On the other hand, when the *glory* of God comes, the flesh doesn't feel very comfortable.

When the glory of God comes, we become like the prophet Isaiah. Our flesh is so weakened by His presence that it is unnecessary for man to do anything other than behold Him in His glory. I've come to the conclusion that, in His presence, I am a man without a vocation. There's no need for me to preach if God shows up in His glory. (See Hebrews 8:11 NIV.) The people are already convinced of His holiness simply by His presence. Simultaneously, they are convicted of their unholiness and their need to repent and live holy before Him. They are aware of His worthiness to receive praise and worship, and they are seized by a driving desire to dive deeper and lead others into His presence!

Jacob prayed and wrestled for a blessing, but what he received was a "changing." His name, his walk, and his demeanor were changed. I'm convinced that, in order to bring godly *change* into our lives, sometimes God puts a little spot of "death" in our bodies (as in Jacob's hip). (See Genesis 32:32.) Something dies within us every time we are confronted by His glory. It's a "handle" for the holy. Just as Isaiah received the hot coals on his lips, we receive the hot bread of His presence and are forever changed. When more of our flesh dies, more of our spirit lives. The first six chapters of Isaiah's prophecy is devoted to "woe." He says, "Woe is me, woe is you, and woe is everybody." But after the prophet saw the Lord high and lifted up, he began to talk about things that can only be understood in the context of the New Testament.

One thing *hasn't changed*: the process of receiving the "blessing" of the hip, or the hot coal of God's glory on our lips of flesh, still doesn't feel good. It still makes us very uncomfortable as we dance around in front of the veil. The priests of old instinctively knew that God's glory wasn't something to trifle with. That is why they tied a rope around the high priest's ankle before he passed through the veil. They knew that if he entered God's presence in presumption or sin, then he wouldn't be walking out of there. They would have to drag his dead body back into our realm outside the veil and hope things would go better the next time. We must face some of the same issues today as we obey God's call for the Church to move from the anointing into His manifest glory.

Tommy Tenney – *The God Chasers*

Take the Bloody Beaten Path to the Mercy Seat

O nly the blood of Christ can purge us from "dead works of the flesh." Could that sense of dullness in our Christian lives and service come from our lack of knowledge about the bloody beaten path to the mercy seat? Trust God's Word. You will come alive to Him if you will allow the blood of Christ to cut away that old deadness and dullness. When you are inundated with the blood of the Lamb, you will finally be like the little bird who escaped bondage and death to break loose and experience true freedom.

It is time for us to find a place at the bloody altar and identify ourselves with the Lamb of God. It is here that we will renew our experience with Him in prayer. Prayers are answered through the blood. It can still destroy plagues, stop demons, and mark a divine dividing line between the holy and the profane, the repentant and the proud.

We must put away the plagues created by our murmuring and lethargy, by our unwilling ways and lack of concern. It is time to die to self and live in Him; it is time to be baptized in the cleansing blood of Christ and the water of the Holy Spirit at an old-fashioned altar of prayer. We must journey to the cross and say before the Lord, "I accept all that is of God. I refuse all that is not of God. I put it all under the blood of the Lord Jesus Christ."

The writer of Hebrews declared:

*Therefore, brethren, having boldness to enter the Holiest **by the blood of Jesus, by a new and living way** which He consecrated for us, through the veil, that is, His flesh, and* *having a High Priest over the house of God, let us draw near with a true heart in full assurance of faith, having our hearts sprinkled from an evil conscience and our bodies washed with pure water (Hebrews 10:19-22 NKJV).*

The way of the blood, the path of the cross, is not a dead way. Unlike the churches man has built using the pattern of the Law and human whims, the true Church is not a way of drudgery and tradition. The Lamb has been slain, the blood was shed, and the "veil" of His flesh was rent.

We are told that when Jesus died, the veil in the temple was rent or torn to *let everyone into the Holiest of Holies.* A careful study of the furniture of the tabernacle reveals that it has always been described from the Holiest of Holies *outward.* Could this be symbolic of God's desire to reach out for humanity, not of humanity reaching for God?

Perhaps Jesus' bloody sacrifice on Calvary was less a way of opening the Holy of Holies to everyone and more a way of God saying, "Let Me out of this little religious box. Let Me get out to where the people are. I am no longer satisfied with the worship and intimate companionship of only one man one time a year. I am after a people, a kingdom of kings and priests...." Maybe this is why the Book of Revelation says of Jesus Christ the Lamb:

You were slain, and have redeemed us to God by Your blood out of every tribe and tongue and people and nation, and have made us kings and priests to our God; and we shall reign on the earth (Revelation 5:9b-10 NKJV).

Jesus' wounded side is open. Blood and water pour forth and you have an invitation to walk through the wound to the very heart of God.

T.F. Tenney and Tommy Tenney – *Secret Sources of Power*

Have You Ever Been
Too Tired to Run?

A re there days when you don't exactly feel like a "God
chaser"? I'm talking about the times when you feel so
"chased" by your own needs and burdens that you can
barely stand up, let alone pursue God.

Since we are humans living in a fallen world, there are times
when even the most determined God chasers among us come to the
heavenly Father loaded down with the heavy burdens of the day. In
our weariness, we reach out for His hand of deliverance or blessing
instead of seeking His face. I know I've been guilty of that!

The Lord understands this and is always gracious toward us.
However, He wants us to know *there is nothing that will lighten our
load or cure our ills* like the indescribable security of gazing upon our
heavenly Father's face and resting in His intimate embrace.

I am just an earthly father who tries to love his children the best
way I can, and I would do almost anything for little Andrea. I also
feel the same way about Tiffany and Natasha, my two older daughters, because they are my children and because they have my favor.

Imagine for a moment what your heavenly Father would do in
your life if you will seek His face instead of only His hands!

When you feel weary beyond words and burdened beyond
despair, I encourage you to remember what Jesus said: "Come unto
Me, all ye that labour and are heavy laden, and I will give you rest"
(Mt. 11:28). This is a divine priority: Seek Him first, and then He will
give you the inward rest that can only come from His presence.

These things began to take on a new significance for me when I received a word from the Lord on the third Sunday of October in 1996 that was simply, "Seek God's face, not His hand." When I searched God's Word, I learned that *to seek God's face means to seek God's favor*. His favor always flows where His face is directed. The reason is simple: God extends His hand wherever He turns His face.

There is a step in our communion with God that goes beyond prayer. It is described in Second Chronicles 7:14: "If My people, which are called by My name, shall humble themselves, and pray, *and seek My face*, and turn from their wicked ways; then will I hear from heaven, and will forgive their sin, and will heal their land."

First we must humble ourselves; then we pray. Then we *seek His face* and confirm our heart change with a life change. The final effect of this promise from God hinges on our obedience to its requirements. If prayer is the biblical act of petitioning and seeking His hand, then seeking God's face is our ultimate act of *positioning*. When we petition for God's face, it eclipses all other requests in God's view.

Esther, the Hebrew maiden-turned-queen, could have petitioned her husband, the king of Persia, from the safety of her quarters in the king's harem. However, she knew that she could only save her nation by risking everything to make a face-to-face entreaty of the king's favor.

Esther prepared herself for 12 months to enter the king's bedchambers and offer herself to him as his bride. She had earned the right to petition the king as his chosen wife, and this was a place of honor. But one day Esther needed more than a formal right of petition. The future of her entire nation was at stake, and she needed a measure of the king's *favor* that could only be found by seeking his face.

Position is important in God's Kingdom. Esther took the risk, entered the king's court, and won the king's favor! A nation was saved! We have a nation to save too.

Will you risk everything to seek the King's face?

GodChasers.network newsletter

Relinquish Your Right to Hurry God

Sometimes God shows you something that will come to pass in the future. If it's not time for it, don't run through the camp shouting, "I'm anointed!" Make sure you relinquish your "right" to hurry God along or to help Him plan out your destiny. He doesn't need our help. God's promises are not tied to time. They are tied to God alone, and He is timeless. He can do a quick work.

If you feel discouraged in this area, remember Moses. When he obeyed God and extended the rod over the Red Sea, the waves split open and the children of Israel walked across to victory. That sounds nice, doesn't it? Now do the math and take courage in God's ability to "hurry things along" when He is ready to do so.

There were between three and five million Israelites, so God didn't struggle to provide a few muddy single-file footpaths for those people. If the Israelites crossed that distance in one night, then they marched five thousand abreast (side by side) along a dry, smooth roadway the width of a 48-lane highway! God opened up the largest freeway in history to get millions of Israelites across the Red Sea, and He did it in a brief period of time. When God gets ready, He can do a quick work. *God delivered the Israelites from four hundred years of bondage in one night!* The Bible says they were "baptized into Moses" (1 Cor. 10:2 NKJV). What a revival! How would you like to see three-to-five million baptized in one night?

God always seems to be interested in what is in our hands. "Mary, what is in your hand?" "An alabaster box of ointment." She broke it open and cast the pieces at the feet of Jesus and now for two thousand years we've been smelling it in the air. That is what release and relinquishment did for her. It was a lasting memorial to Jesus' death on the cross.

No one else noticed, but Jesus saw what was in the widow's hand when she dropped her last two mites into the offering plate. He honored her as an example of the kind of sacrificial giving God loves to bless, and her example has been utilized to build the faith of believers and raise millions of dollars for the Kingdom of God over the centuries. It was all because this widow took what was in her hand and relinquished it to the Lord by faith. Like the song says, "Little is much when God is in it."

We must have the spirit of selflessness manifested in the prayers Jesus taught us to pray and modeled before us: "Nevertheless not My will, but Yours, be done" (Lk. 22:42b NKJV). "Your kingdom come. Your will be done on earth as it is in heaven" (Mt. 6:10 NKJV).

T.F. Tenney and Tommy Tenney – *Secret Sources of Power*

Sometimes We Can Stop Short

S ome of us seem to thrive on the momentary revelations of God when He wants us to press in for His secret things. He loves to honor the prayers of persistent pursuers like Moses, but He will actually stop our attempts to build monuments to partial and incomplete revelations of His glory—especially ones that we never paid for with our prayers and death on the altar of brokenness. We like things to come quickly, easily, and cheaply— *microwave revival.* God knows that such things never produce godly character in us. He says:

> *...If any man will come after Me, let him deny himself, and take up his cross, and follow Me.*
>
> *For whosoever will save his life shall lose it: and whosoever will lose his life for My sake shall find it.*
>
> *For what is a man profited, if he shall gain the whole world, and lose his own soul? or what shall a man give in exchange for his soul? (Matthew 16:24-26).*

I have feebly tried to explain the unexplainable, but all I know is this: *"The more I die, the closer God gets."* I don't know how much of God you know or have, but He will reveal *more* of Himself to you if you are willing to die to yourself. Paul the apostle said he knew a man (himself) who was caught up into the third heaven in Second Corinthians 12:2. This apostle didn't merely know "about" God; he *knew God.* How did he gain that intimate knowledge? He said, "I die daily" (see 1 Cor. 15:31).

Many modern saints spend a lot of time looking for shortcuts to God's glory. *We want the gain without the pain.* We want revival in our cities, but we don't want to hear anyone tell us that revival only comes when people are hungry, when "vicarious intercessors" repent for sins they never committed on behalf of people they've never met. Paul said, "For I could wish that myself were accursed from Christ for my brethren, my kinsmen according to the flesh" (Rom. 9:3).

You are reading this book by divine appointment. Somewhere, somehow, an unforgettable prayer is being answered today. But it could be that you are avoiding death and you're running from the altar of sacrifice that God has placed before you. (Don't worry, it is true of *all* of us.) The greatest blessing doesn't come from God's hand; it comes from His face in intimate relationship. You find the true source of all power when you finally see Him and *know* Him in His glory.

Now let me tell you the good news beyond the altar of death and brokenness. While all flesh dies in His glory, all that is of the Spirit *lives forever* in His glory. That part of your being that really wants to live can live forever, but something about your flesh has to die. Let me put it this way: *Your flesh holds back the glory of God.* The God of Moses is willing to reveal Himself to you today, but it is not going to be a "cheap" blessing. You're going to have to lay down and die, and *the more you die, the closer He can come.*

You need to forget about the opinions and expectations of those around you. You need to lay aside every idea of what the "normal religious protocol" may be. God has only one protocol for the flesh: *death.* God is out to redefine the Church. He is sending His fire to burn away everything that isn't from Him anyway, so you have nothing to lose...but your flesh. God isn't looking for religious people; He's looking for people who are hot after His heart. He wants people who want Him, who want the Blesser more than the blessings.

We can seek for His blessing and play with His toys, or we can say, "No, Father, we don't just want the blessings; we want *You.* We want You to come close. Touch our eyes. Touch our hearts and ears. Change us, Lord. We are tired of the way we are. We understand that if we can change, then our city and nation can change."

Tommy Tenney – *The God Chasers*

The Confession of People in Love

hese kinds of believers don't gauge their relationship with God by whether they received a salary raise this quarter, by how things are going with their bank account, or by how much "fun" they've had during church activities. They have joined Paul by saying, "But none of these things move me, *neither count I my life dear unto myself,* so that I might finish my course with joy, and the ministry, which I have received of the Lord Jesus, to testify the gospel of the grace of God" (Acts 20:24). This is the confession of people in love and in intimate communion with their Maker.

God is calling. The first time God revealed this to me, I trembled and wept in front of the people as I told them the same thing I tell you today: "You are at Mount Sinai today, and God is calling you into personal intimacy with Him. If you dare to answer His call, then it is going to redefine everything you've ever done." Your decision today will determine whether you go forward or backward in your walk with Christ.

Intimacy with God requires a certain level of brokenness because purity comes from brokenness. The games are over, friend. He's calling you.

Could it be that we don't want to get into that cloud with God because we know He's going to look into our hearts, and we know what He will find there? We have to deal with more than our outward actions; we have to deal with our inward motives also. We must come clean, because God can't reveal His face to a partially pure Church. It would be destroyed in an instant.

God is calling people who want serious revival into a place of transparent purity. It's *you* who He's after. He wants you to draw near, but at the same time, if you come near, then He will have to deal with you. That can only mean one thing: You must die. This is the same God who told Moses, "No man has seen My face and lived." So remember to pass by the altar of forgiveness and sacrifice on your way into the Holy of Holies. It's time for us to lay our egos on the cross, to crucify our will, to lay our own agendas aside.

God is calling you to a higher level of commitment. Forget the plans you've made for yourself and lay on His altar and die to self. Pray, "God, what do You want me to do?" It's time to lay everything aside and cover yourself in the blood. Nothing alive can stand in His presence. But if you're dead, then He will make you alive. So all you need to do is die if you really want to get into His presence. When the apostle Paul wrote, "I die daily," he was saying, "I enter into the presence of God every day" (see 1 Cor. 15:31b). Run in, don't run away!

Tommy Tenney – *The God Chasers*

Are You Always on God's Mind?

esus said that this woman who had broken her alabaster box to anoint Him for His burial would never be forgotten wherever the gospel is preached. In other words, *she would always be on God's mind.* Do you want a visitation from God? You will have to make room for Him in your life, no matter how crowded and cluttered it may be at this moment. Sometimes it means your most treasured things may have to be broken to release the fragrance God remembers.

Your brokenness is a sweet-smelling savor to God. He collects every tear that drips from your chin and flows from the corners of your eyes. The Bible says that He has a bottle of memories to hold every tear you've shed. (See Psalm 56:8.) He loves you, so steal away to your secret prayer place and pull out that "alabaster box" of precious anointing you've been saving for such a time as this. Break it at His feet and say, "Jesus, I love You more than anything. I'll give up anything; I'll go anywhere. I just want You, Lord."

Make no mistake, it took humility for Mary to wipe the Lord's feet with her hair. The Bible says a woman's hair is her glory (see 1 Cor. 11:15), so Mary used her glory to wipe the feet of Jesus. Middle Eastern women in Jesus' day generally wore their hair "up," and it was often wrapped in a turban or veil when they left their homes for public places. So Mary probably had to unwrap or "dismantle" her hair to wipe the Lord's feet. I don't want to offend anyone, but it is important for us to understand what that really meant to Mary's reputation. Open sandals were the most common footwear, and it was customary for guests to leave their sandals at the door when they entered a house. Since most travelers in Israel shared the main roads with camels, horses, and donkeys, it was impossible to completely avoid the droppings of these animals all day long.

Sandals provided some protection to travelers, and it was unthinkable to wear them into a person's house. Nevertheless, it was certain that the residue of the day's journey (including the odor of the animal droppings) was still deposited on a guest's unprotected feet. For this reason, the dirty job of washing the animal droppings off of everyone's feet was reserved for the most insignificant servant of the household. Any servant who washed a guest's feet was automatically considered the one "who doesn't count, the unimportant expendable slave," and was openly treated with disdain.

What a picture of humble worship Mary provides. She dismantled her "glory," her hair, to wipe animal waste from His feet. Our righteousness and glory are nothing but filthy rags, fit only to wipe His feet! (See Isaiah 64:6.)

If you really wanted to dishonor and humiliate a person who entered your home, all you had to do was make sure that your servants didn't bother to wash his feet. This was especially true in a Pharisee's house where outward cleanliness meant everything. Jesus clearly says that when He entered Simon's house, no one washed His feet (refer to Luke 7:44). It is almost like Simon wanted Jesus there, but he didn't want to honor Him. How often do we want God present in our services but refuse (or ignore) to worship Him as we should?

Tommy Tenney – *Extreme GodChasers*

An Anointer or the Anointed

We "pedestalize" people whom God has anointed. Whom does God memorialize? Jesus says that what Mary did will "be told for a memorial of her" (Mt. 26:13). We like the anointed; He likes the "anointers"! These are people of His face and feet—oil pourers, tear washers, humble lovers of Him more than lovers of His things.

I believe that Mary actually anointed Jesus *twice*, and was going to anoint Him a third time. First she came as a sinner and anointed His feet, longing to receive forgiveness at any cost in Luke chapter 7. Then she anointed His head at the end of His earthly ministry in Matthew chapter 26 and Mark chapter 14. Jesus Himself said that she did it "for My burial" (Mt. 26:12). Just think of it. He's hanging on the cross, suspended between Heaven and earth as though unworthy of both, abandoned by all, breathing His last agonizing breaths.

But what's that He smells...more than the salty smell of blood trickling down His fractured face, stronger than the noise of dice thrown by the soldiers, overpowering the jeers of the Jewish priests? *It's the fragrance of past worship, captured in the locks of His hair...He smells the oil from the alabaster box!* The memory of the worship of an "anointer" strengthens His resolve, and He "finishes" the task at hand.

This same woman who anointed Him in His life witnessed the crucifixion and said, "I can't leave Him unanointed in His death." As she carried yet another compound of precious spices to anoint the Lord's body in the tomb, she found His tomb empty and again felt her heart break with emptiness as she began to bitterly weep and cry. Oh, the love of an anointer! They are willing even to pour anointing over dead dreams!

Jesus had just vacated the tomb and was on His way to sprinkle His shed blood on the mercy seat when He heard her familiar cry. This was potentially the most important task that Jesus ever did, because it was the heavenly fulfillment of the most important task that any earthly high priest ever did in his sanctity and cleanliness. The high priests of Israel had to be very careful to avoid becoming ceremonially defiled, so no woman was allowed to touch them at all. Yet just as Jesus began His ascent on high to sprinkle His blood on the true mercy seat in Heaven, He saw the one who had dismantled her glory to clean His feet, *the anointer*. Perhaps He had one foot on the bottom rung of Jacob's ladder that ascends into Heaven when He abruptly stopped and said, "She's come to do it again. She has come with her precious fragrances and sacrifices of praise, only I am not there to receive it." So He stopped on His way to do the most important task He would ever do and said, "I can't leave her here without letting her know."

You can literally arrest the purposes and plans of God if you are a worshiper. Jesus stopped what He was doing to go to a person who had broken her most precious alabaster box to anoint Him. He stopped when He saw her tears and went to stand behind her. Finally He said, "Mary, Mary."

What made the Son of God do that? Why did the great High Priest of Heaven stop His advance toward the mercy seat for the cries of a former prostitute? I can tell you this: *He only does it for "hall-of-famers."* At first Mary didn't even recognize Him because He had changed. She said, "Where have you put Him? Where have you put the familiar appearance I've grown used to seeing?" She thought the glorified Christ was just the gardener (*sounds like many of us today who often fail to recognize God's glory when it stares us in the face*).

Finally Mary stopped her sobbing enough to really hear His voice as He said, "Mary." His likeness had been changed from mortal to immortal, and His whole countenance had been altered from something of this world to something that was not of this world. He quickly said, "Mary, don't touch Me. I really don't want to go through all that sacrifice on the cross all over again, so don't touch Me. But Mary, I just had to let you know that I am all right. Go tell the disciples." (See John 20k:17.) *He **had** to tell her **not** to touch Him*; it's as though He knew she would for Him to say this! He also had to be near enough for her to touch Him if she wished to. *It was as if Jesus would have risked being defiled as High Priest for the sake of a worshiper.*

God will whisper His prophetic secrets before they ever come to pass for broken-box worshipers and fragrant anointers. He will turn aside at the height of His glory for people who will dismantle their own glory and ego just to share His shame as their own.

Tommy Tenney – *The God Chasers*

Disaster or Miracle? Follow the Spirit!

S ome of the most embarrassing moments in a minister's life may be those times when he or she tried to "rebuke" something only to find out that it was God at work. Form must always follow function. Many local churches expect the Holy Spirit to conform to their order of service, printed church schedule, or pre-established agendas; when all of those outward forms should follow the leading of the Spirit. Many times, what we think is the beginning of a disaster will actually be the beginning of a miracle! This happens most often when we fail to discern the seasons of the Lord. There are times to hold on and there are times to let things go. In the same way, there is a time and a season for "unloading."

Jonathan made a spiritual covenant with David and their hearts were knit together. Yet he also had a physical covenant with his father. He was torn between his loyalty to his spiritual brother and his biological father, King Saul. When he followed the flesh instead of the spiritual, early death came to him. (See 1 Samuel 31:2.) He could not discern what to hold and what to unload.

Finally, we must realize that before there can be a filling, there has to be an emptying. It is hard for God to fill a person who is already running over with "self." He can't give you solutions when you are clinging to your problems and refuse to unload them.

Sometimes we have to unload the assignments we cannot accomplish by ourselves. God told the prophet Elijah to do three specific tasks, but he only accomplished one of those assignments—the anointing of Elisha. (See 1 Kings 19:15-16.) God passed the remaining assignments on to Elisha after Elijah was caught up into heaven. Elijah felt the burden of three generations during his ministry. God knew Elijah could not fulfill all three tasks, so He just transferred the burden to another. You will always sense the "burden of the unfulfilled" if you are part of God's eternal purpose. Just remember there are times when you must release your burden to future generations.

When you sense there are eternal things you will never accomplish in your lifetime, you have a choice: You can become frustrated by it, or you can realize that things are either *timely* or *timeless*. God speaks both into our hearts. Our job is to know what to unload, what to fulfill, and what to pass on.

There will be times when you simply need to unload. Get with God, rest in the Father, worship Jesus, and walk in the Spirit. Love Him. Serve Him. Do your best to please Him, and remember that if something pleases God, it doesn't matter who it displeases. If it displeases Him, it doesn't matter who else is pleased.

If you want God to infuse you with last-day revival power, then understand that first you may need to unload some things in your life. He may be waiting for you to get rid of some things to make room for Him. Do you love Him beyond everything and everyone else? Do you love Him more than any problem or position in your life? Do you focus on Him more than the distractions in your life? Is He greater than every failure and disappointment you have experienced? Lay aside the weights...lay aside the sins that so easily entangle you...*consider Him.* This is the first step on the road to power.

T.F. Tenney and Tommy Tenney – *Secret Sources of Power*

Stopping Short and Missing Out

Some may call it blasphemy, but I must tell you that I have attended enough "good church services" to last me a lifetime. "Good" just isn't good enough anymore. I don't want to hear any more "good" singing and I don't even want to hear any more "good" preaching. In fact, I am bored with myself! Would you be interested in tasting something "good" when you know the "best" is waiting in the kitchen?

I know my comments sound extreme, but they are mild when placed in the context of what I really desire: I want God to show up in His *shekinah* or tangible glory. Compared to Him, everything and everyone else is reduced to a warm-up act filling time until the Real Thing enters the room. I am afraid that we have built a religion and a lifestyle around the appetizers while completely forgetting the main course!

We experience a taste or a fleeting hint of God's glory every time we find ourselves in places where what we call "revival" has broken out. Since this "glory" is a "spirit thing," it defies scientific definition or quantifiable verification. Instead there is a certain "feeling" or inner sense of God's approaching presence that warns us something very large and powerful is drawing near.

When this happens, we tend to handle the situation much of the time like inexperienced runners in a sprint race. We explode from the blocks in eager pursuit of God's presence and continue at a fast pace until we begin to feel the discomfort of an all-consuming hunt for the trophy of our heart's desire.

Some of us feel our strength failing and our senses becoming dull to things around us as we gasp for breath. With one last burst of desperate energy we stretch forward and lunge toward the line...only to stumble forward and fall several yards *short* of the finish line. By stopping too soon, by failing to press forward all the way through to the finish, *we are racing to false finish lines and fail to seize the prize.*

The Bible tells us that on a mountaintop in Israel, three disciples sleepily cracked open their eyes just enough to see Moses and Elijah standing with Jesus in a cloud of glory. (See Luke 9:28-32.) The disciples suddenly woke up and Peter interrupted the Son of God to suggest that everyone stop at the false finish line to build a monument to the event. Peter used the term *rabbi*, or teacher, when he spoke to Jesus, and he suggested building three separate structures as if he possibly felt that Moses and Elijah were equal to Jesus. Perhaps he had no idea that the best was yet to come.

Moses had waited more than ten lifetimes to see what was about to come to pass, and I doubt that he was interested in Peter's false finish line. He wanted nothing less than to see God's glory revealed. Then the Father interrupted Peter while he was still talking and corrected the disciple's earthbound perspective when He said, "This is My Son, whom I have chosen; listen to Him" (Lk. 9:35b). Then everything and every person faded from sight except the exalted Lord of all.

Too often we stop at false finish lines because our flesh gets excited. We want to interrupt God's revelation of Himself so we can build sand castles in honor of the first premonition of His appearing. We are so busy saying, "It is good we are here," that we don't hear God say, "I want to join you there too."

Tommy Tenney – *God's Favorite House*

People Leave the House of Bread for One Reason

Naomi and her husband and two sons left home and moved to Moab *because there was a famine in Bethlehem.* Consider the literal meaning of the Hebrew name of their hometown: Bethlehem means "house of bread." The reason they left the *house of bread* is that there was *no bread in the house.* It's simple, why people leave churches—there's no bread. Bread was part of the temple practices as well; it was proof of His presence—the *showbread,* the bread of the presence. Bread has always been the one thing historically that was an indicator of His presence. We find in the Old Testament that bread in the form of the showbread was in the Holy Place. It was called "the bread of the Presence" (Num. 4:7 NRSV). Showbread might better be interpreted as "show up bread," or in the Hebraic terms, "face bread." It was a heavenly symbol of God Himself.

Naomi and her family have something in common with the people who leave or totally avoid our churches today—they left *"that"* place and went somewhere else to try to find bread. I can tell you why people are flocking to the bars, the clubs, and the psychics by the millions. They're just trying to get by; they are just trying to survive because the Church has failed them. They looked, or their parents and friends looked and reported, and the spiritual cupboard was bare. There was no presence in the pantry; just empty shelves and offices full of recipes for bread. But the oven was cold and dusty.

We have falsely advertised and hyped-up our claims that there is bread in our house. But when the hungry come, all they can do is scrounge through the carpet for a few crumbs of yesteryears' revivals. We talk grandly about where He has been and what He has done, but we can say very little about what He is doing among us today. That isn't God's fault; it is ours. We have only remnants of what used to be—a residue of the fading glory. And unfortunately, we keep the veil of secrecy over that fact, much in the same way Moses kept the veil over his face after the shine of "glory dust" faded. (See 2 Corinthians 3:13 NIV.) We camouflage our emptiness like the priesthood in Jesus' day kept the veil in place with no ark of the covenant behind it.

God may have to "pierce" the veil of our flesh to reveal our (the Church's) inner emptiness also. It's a pride problem—we point with pride to where He has been (protecting the temple tradition) while we deny the obviously apparent "glory" of the Son of God. The religious spirits of Jesus' day didn't want the populace to realize that there was no glory behind their veil. Jesus' presence presented problems. Religious spirits must preserve where He's been at the expense of where He is!

But a man with an experience is never at the mercy of a man with only an argument. "All I know is I was blind but now I see!" (See John 9:25.) If we can lead people into the manifest presence of God, all false theological houses of cards will tumble down.

Yet we wonder why people hardly bow their heads when they come in our meetings and places of worship. "Where has the fear of God gone?" we cry like A.W. Tozer. People don't sense God's presence in our gatherings because it's just not there sufficiently enough to register on our gauges. This, in turn, creates another problem. When people get just a little touch of God mixed with a lot of something that is not God, it inoculates them against the real thing. Once they've been "inoculated" by a crumb of God's presence, then when we say, "God really is here"; they say, "No, I've been there, done that. I bought that T-shirt, and I didn't find Him; it really didn't work for me." The problem is that God was there all right, but not enough of Him! There was no experience of meeting Him at the Damascus road. There was no undeniable, overwhelming sense of His manifest presence.

People have come to the House of Bread time and again only to find there was simply *too much of man* and *too little of God* there. The Almighty One is out to restore the sense of His awesome manifest presence in our lives and places of worship. Over and over we talk about the glory of God covering the earth, but how is it going to flow through the streets of our cities if it can't even flow down the aisles of our churches? It's got to start somewhere, and it's not going to start out "there." It must start in "here"! It must start at "the temple," as Ezekiel wrote. "...I saw water coming out from under the threshold of the temple..." (Ezek. 47:1 NIV).

If God's glory can't flow through the aisles of the church because of seducing spirits and manipulating men, then God will have to turn somewhere else as He did the day Jesus rode past "the house of bread" (temple) in Jerusalem on a donkey. If there is no bread in the house, then I don't blame the hungry for not going there! I wouldn't!

Tommy Tenney – *The God Chasers*

The Temptation Is to Promise Him When You Can't Deliver Him

*W*e have practiced and perfected the art of entertaining man, but along the way we have lost the art of entertaining God. We've already talked about the weeping zone, that place of priestly intercession between the court of man and the altar of God where we reach toward God with one hand and reach toward man with the other. Sometimes we get so involved in attracting man to our outstretched hand that we lose the desire and the ability to attract God with the other. When you can pull men toward you but you can't get God to come close anymore, the temptation is to keep promising Him though you can't deliver Him.

Time and again we gather large crowds of people under a plastic banner that proclaims, "Revival!" Then we become like some perpetual late night TV co-host of the church scene, saying, "Here's God!" With practiced voice inflection and hand flourishes we invite and announce Him—only we have no place for Him to sit. In our drive to please men we forgot to please God. *There's no mercy seat!*

So He never really quite shows up. He just peeps out from behind the curtains (or the lattice, as Solomon said), releasing just enough of His anointing to let you know He's there, but not enough to have a Damascus Road encounter that utterly changes you.

Part of the problem is our habit of misusing terminology to artificially raise the expectations of people. *We perpetually over-promise and under-produce.* As I said before, if someone says, *"The glory of God is here"* from an upright position, you have my permission to question the validity of the comment. We are guilty of hyping trickles into torrents—but only in our vain imaginations. When people from the world walk in, they say, "It's nice in here. It feels peaceful. Good, it is God. There's no doubt about it, it's God...*but how much of God?*" And then they walk out.

We promise God's glory, but often at best we give a limited measure of God's anointing. God's anointing was never meant to satisfy the hunger of our souls. The anointing and the gifts empowered by it are simply tools to assist, enable, encourage, and point us back to their Source. Only God Himself can satisfy the hunger He placed within us. *His hand can supply our needs, but only His face can satisfy our deepest longings.* As we look upon His face, we are brought into union with our destiny, and we enjoy the favor of His loving gaze and the incomparable kiss of His lips.

There is a big difference between encountering the anointing of God and encountering His glory. I'm not really interested in the anointing anymore—not when it is compared to the glory of His manifest presence. I say that because it is the only way I know to help people understand the dramatic difference between the anointing and the glory of God.

The anointing of God in all its various forms has a valid purpose in His plans and purposes. The problem is that we have become so addicted to the way the anointing makes us feel that we've turned our eyes and hearts away from the glory of God's face to get more of the anointing in His hands. The anointing empowers our flesh, and it makes us feel good. *That is why the Church is filled with "anointing junkies"* on **both** *sides of the pulpit.* Most (but not all) the antics in our services that draw fire from the world and various segments of the Church can be traced to this odd addiction.

If you don't believe me, ask yourself why people will trample one another to get a "hot spot" in the prayer line at major conferences.

Explain to me why born-again Christians will lie, scheme, and break every rule in the book to get the "best seats" in the convention hall when "Hot Evangelist What's His Name" comes to town? Honestly, there are a lot of nationally known preachers who have fan clubs nowadays. They don't call them fan clubs, of course, because that would be embarrassing, but it is true nonetheless. *This is typical behavior when preachers and their fans become addicted to the power of the anointing.*

Tommy Tenney – *God's Favorite House*

Whatever Happened to the Bread?

The sign is still up. We still take people into our churches and show them the ovens where we used to bake bread. The ovens are all still in place and everything is there, but all you can find is crumbs from last year's visitation, and from the last great wave of revival our predecessors talked about. Now we are reduced to being shallow students of what we hope to experience some day. I'm constantly reading about revival, and God impressed upon me recently, "Son, you're reading about it because *you don't yet have the experience to write about.*"

I am tired of reading *about* God's visitations of yesteryear. I want God to break out somewhere in my lifetime so that in the future my children can say, "*I was there.* I know; it's true." God has no grandchildren. Each generation must experience His presence. Recitation was never meant to take the place of visitation.

Two things happen when the bread of God's presence is restored to the Church. Naomi was a prodigal who left the house of bread when that table became bare. Yet once she heard that God had restored bread to Bethlehem, the house of bread, she quickly returned. *The prodigals will come walking back into Bethlehem* from Moab once they know there is bread in the house, and *they won't come alone.* Naomi came back to the house of bread accompanied by Ruth, who had never been there before. The never saved will come. As a result, Ruth became part of the Messianic lineage of Jesus when she married Boaz and bore him a son named Obed, who was the father of Jesse, the father of David. (See Ruth 4:17.) Future royalty awaits our hunger-spurred actions.

Revival as we know it "*now*" is really the "recycling" of saved people through the Church to keep them fired up. But the next wave of true revival will bring waves of unchurched people into the House of Bread—people who have never darkened the door of a church in their lives. When they hear that there really is bread in the house, they will stream through our doors after smelling the fragrance of hot bread from the ovens of Heaven!

Often we are so full and satisfied with other things that we insist on "getting by" with our crumbs of the past. We're happy with our music the way it is. We're happy with our "renewal" meetings. It is time for some of what I have politely termed "divine discontent." Can I say it and not be judged? *I'm not happy.* By that I mean that even though I have been a participant in what some would call the revival of a lifetime, I am still not happy. Why? Because I know what *can* happen. I can catch Him. I know that there is far more than anything we have seen or hoped for yet, and it has become a holy obsession. I want God. I want more of Him.

Tommy Tenney – *Extreme GodChasers*

We Prostitute the Anointing Because We Want to Smell Good

The primary purpose of the anointing in both the Old and New Testaments was to separate things and people and make them acceptable to God (and occasionally for kings). Unfortunately, we tend to prostitute the anointing because we want to smell good for everybody else.

According to the second chapter of the Book of Esther, after the wife of King Ahasuerus of Persia refused to show herself to his drunken banquet guests, he launched a kingdom-wide search for a new queen. A Jewish maiden named Esther was selected to be one of the candidates for the king's harem. As I said in *The God Chasers*, Esther and the other prospective brides spent "one year in preparation for one night with the king" (Tommy Tenney, *The God Chasers* [Shippensburg, PA: Destiny Image Publishers, 1998], 41).

Esther spent six months soaking in oil of myrrh and six more months soaking in other added sweet odors to purify and prepare her for one night with the king. All but one of the candidates would see the king once and rarely if ever see him again. The Bible says, "And the king loved Esther above all the women, and she obtained *grace* and *favour* in his sight more than all the virgins; so that he set the royal crown upon her head, and made her queen..." (Esther 2:17).

Esther also "obtained *favour* in the sight of all them that looked upon her" (Esther 2:15). Can you imagine what Esther smelled like after spending a year soaking in the anointing oil? It was on her garments and embedded in her skin and hair. Everywhere she walked she left a cloud of incense, and the smell of precious myrrh was on her. When she walked through the palace, every man in the place raised his eyebrows at her and said, "Oh, look! Look at Esther."

I don't think Esther returned a single glance or flirtatious wink. She didn't want to waste all the time she had spent in the anointing just to win the approval of men; *she was after the approval of the king himself.* Can we say the same for the Church, the Bride of Christ? We have grown accustomed to wearing God's anointing to win the approval of the King's court instead of the King Himself. In Moses' day, the anointing was reserved for the things of God and sanctified or set apart flesh. To anoint anything else was sin. Too many people would squander the anointing on unsanctified, unrepentant flesh to win man's approval. *The anointing can only make putrified flesh smell better temporarily if the root is a rotten and unrepentant, proud heart.*

If you are a preacher, a teacher, a worship leader, or hold any position of responsibility in the local body, don't waste God's precious anointing by running after man's approval. Use it to prepare the Bride for the King.

The purpose of the anointing is to bring God and man together in holy communion. Moses knew the difference between the anointing and the glory. He had the anointing of God. He knew the thrill of working miracles and signs and wonders through the anointing. Moses had a good thing, but he asked God for the best thing. He said, "Please, show me Your *glory*" (Ex. 33:18 NKJV).

I must admit, I feel the same way Moses did (although I won't compare my ministry to his). The evidence of God's power in the anointing isn't enough anymore. The gifts, blessings, and provisions of His hands are appreciated, but I want more. **I want Him.** *I long to see His glory and dwell in His manifest presence more than I long for the blessings of His hands.*

Like Moses, we have an opportunity to go beyond God's omnipresence and anointing to see God's glory. Our spirits were instantly transformed into new creations at salvation, but we still need to do something about our sin-tainted bodies and messy souls before God can expose us to His shining glory. The blood of Jesus covers our sin and preserves us from death, but that doesn't mean we are particularly attractive to God apart from the fragrant covering cloud of repentant, broken worship.

Tommy Tenney – *God's Favorite House*

Don't Dig Up Old Offenses—Release Your Debtors Forever

When the people of Jerusalem re-enslaved their brethren and canceled their forgiveness, the armies of Nebuchadnezzar came back and gave them exactly what they had given each other. The former "owners" were carried off to Babylon as slaves while their former slaves remained behind to take possession of their land and belongings. How many times have we forgiven a brother or sister in Christ only to go "dig up" their offense again and place them back into the slavery of our unforgiveness? God *still* notes it.

Are you prepared if God suddenly calls for an "audit" of your conduct toward your brothers and sisters? Remember that He doesn't need an audit—He already sees and knows all things. He holds each of us personally responsible for forgiving others, with no exceptions to the rule. We were not created or designed to carry bitterness and unforgiveness in our hearts. It is like trying to carry battery acid in a Styrofoam cup—the acid of unforgiveness eats away at every part of our lives.

Jesus said His disciples would be known for their love for one another. Love transcends the "ledger-sheet mentality" that keeps track of every wrong done and offense received. The "God-kind-of-love" described in First Corinthians chapter 13 doesn't keep a score or an "account" of wrongs suffered.

"Mercy [always] triumphs over judgment" (Jas. 2:13b), so operate in love and "set your slaves free." Release the power of forgiveness in your life. God is saying, "If you show mercy to others, I will show you mercy."

We also need to learn how to *forgive ourselves.* It is difficult to keep Jesus' command to "love others as we love ourselves" when we really don't love ourselves. Many times, self-hatred or inner resentments build up because of our fear of failure or rejection.

T.F. Tenney and Tommy Tenney – *Secret Sources of Power*

America Is Hungry, but the Bread Is Stale

Frankly, we would be totally unable to contain or manage such a harvest of souls in our present state because we don't have enough fresh bread of His presence on our shelves for the hungry masses! It may bother some people that I say that, but I have a problem with our "part-time, gone fishing" church mentality. We touched on this earlier in Chapter 2, "No Bread in the 'House of Bread,' " but it bears repeating until the situation changes. Why is it that on every corner in America's cities we have little convenience stores *that stay open 24 hours a day* just to meet the public's demand for their goods? Meanwhile, most of America's churches supposedly satisfy the nation's hunger for God while operating only two hours a week on Sunday morning! Why isn't the Church staying open every night and day? Aren't we supposed to be offering the Bread of Life to the hungry? Something is terribly wrong, and I don't think it is America's hunger for God. They are hungry all right, but they are smart enough to tell the difference between the stale bread of yesterday's religious experience and the fresh bread of God's genuine presence. Once again we must conclude that the reason the hungry aren't knocking on our doors is because the House of Bread is empty.

It is interesting to note that not one of the 50 largest churches in the world is in the United States. "How can that be? Haven't we sent missionaries around the world for more than 200 years?" The hungry need fresh bread in abundance, not stale crumbs in the carpet from last century's wedding rehearsal dinner.

I have a friend who pastors a church of about 7,000 believers. His church is arguably the best cell-based model church in America, but he told me that he had recently attended a conference overseas and what he discovered there brought tears to his eyes.

He told me, "Tommy, there's something that just really griped me at that conference." He explained that the conference sponsored a workshop for pastors who pastored churches larger than 100,000, and then he said, "I couldn't stand it. I just had to open the door and stick my head into that meeting to see if there was anybody there. The room had about 20 or 30 people in it, and it just griped me that I couldn't go in there." Then with tears in his eyes, he told me, "Then it dawned on me, Tommy. Nobody in that room was an American."

This man has been fairly successful by American standards. He has managed to make a sizable dent on his city of about 400,000, but he wants to do *more*. He isn't a head-counter or a number-chaser who is interested only in competing with other pastors who brag about their Sunday morning attendance figures. He is a God chaser and a soulwinner. His tears weren't tears of jealousy; they were tears of sorrow. If there has ever been a country ripe for revival, it is the United States. It is time for God's people to get desperately hungry after Him, because the fires of revival must first ignite the Church before its flames can spread to the streets.

I am weary of trying to accomplish God's works with the hands of man. What we need for nationwide revival is one thing and one thing only: *We need to have God show up.*

If you want your local high school classes to turn into prayer meetings, then you will need to see God show up. I'm not talking about a theoretical or historical occurrence. There have been times when God's glory has been flowing in His churches so much that His people had to be careful in area restaurants. Simply bowing their heads to pray over their meal, they look up to see waitresses and other customers all around, just weeping uncontrollably and saying, "*What is it* with you people?"

My wife was standing in line to pay for some purchases at a store during God's visitation in Houston when a lady tapped her on the shoulder. She turned around to see who it was to find a total stranger weeping unashamedly. This lady told my wife, "I don't know where you've been, and I don't know what you've got. But my husband is a lawyer and I'm in the middle of a divorce." She began to blurt out her other problems and finally said, "What I'm really saying is, *I need God.*"

My wife looked around and said, "You mean right here?"

She said, "Right here."

My wife just had to ask again, "Well, what about the people in line?"

Suddenly the lady turned to the woman standing in line behind her and said, "Ma'am, is it okay if I pray with this lady right here?"

But that lady was also crying and she said, "Yes, and pray with me too."

Tommy Tenney – *The God Chasers*

Do Your Actions Glorify What Satan Stands For?

S atan is attracted by any atmosphere that has one or more of his own characteristics. People don't realize they can easily create an atmosphere that attracts him by doing things that glorify what he stands for.

We know that we can create an atmosphere that attracts the Holy Spirit or grieves and repulses Him. God's Word tells us to, "Enter into His gates with thanksgiving, and into His courts with praise. Be thankful to Him, and bless His name" (Ps. 100:4). When we thank the Lord, praise Him, and bless His name, we find ourselves in His presence. It is a question of attitude.

What attitudes create a comfortable place for satan? We know the actions and activities of the King of Tyre created such a comfortable atmosphere for satan that he took up residence behind his throne and empowered the king to do his evil bidding.

Many of the evil things happening in our day are not merely the work of flesh and blood. Paul warned us not to fight on the "wrong front." He said, "We do not wrestle against flesh and blood, but against principalities, against powers, against the rulers of the darkness of this age, against spiritual hosts of wickedness in the heavenly places" (Eph. 6:12). We don't need to "look for a demon under every rock," but much of the evil that appears to be human activity alone is motivated, directed, and even empowered by demonic principalities, powers, and spiritual wickedness in high places.

Evil human attitudes and actions create a welcoming "comfort zone" or atmosphere where the enemy can work even greater demonic evil in comfort and concealment. An atmosphere of disunity is especially attractive to the enemy because it *empowers* him. When people get in disunity, they commit spiritual treason and their actions weaken God's Kingdom and strengthen satan's position. He constantly works to make us believe our real battle is against other people, but his favorite tactic is to pit brother against brother in the family of God. When it works, he just hides behind our thrones and laughs. His kingdom is secure for the moment because just as *unity brings revival*, so will *disunity dispel it!*

The Gospels of Matthew and Mark tell us that one day Simon Peter declared Jesus' true identity as the Son of God by revelation of the Holy Spirit, and received Jesus' praise for his discernment. Then Jesus announced that He would die and rise again, and Peter rebuked Him for saying it! He said, "It will never happen to You, Lord! No, sir, we're going to stand with You...." Peter's religious words sounded good. They had the ring of true devotion and sincerity, but they were diabolically wrong.

Simon Peter's pride and presumption created an atmosphere ripe for a satanic visitation. The enemy joined their dinner party and used unsuspecting Peter to proclaim the hopes of hell. Satan must have snickered when Peter told Jesus the Messiah that He was wrong to say He was going to die on the cross. The words had hardly left Peter's mouth before Jesus confronted him. Looking beyond the familiar face of Simon Peter, the Lord directly addressed the evil archangel hiding "behind the throne": "Get behind Me, satan! You are an offense to Me, for you are not mindful of the things of God, but the things of men" (Mt. 16:23b).

There are times when "doing right" by your definition is actually "doing wrong" by God's. Something is "right" when it is lined up with God's Word and confirmed by His Spirit. Peter experienced that when he accurately declared Jesus' true identity. However, he had to completely dismiss the reality of Jesus' identity that he had just discovered in order to say what he did. If Jesus was the Son of God, why would He lie about His destiny?

When your action seems "right" but the way you go about it is wrong, it is the worst kind of "wrongness" because it can deceive and lead others down the wrong path as well. Peter was saying, "You won't die. We will stand by You," but Jesus knew He could never accomplish His purpose on earth without Calvary. Anything that could or would attempt to block the purposes of God could not be from God. *All good ideas are not "God ideas."*

T.F. Tenney and Tommy Tenney – *Secret Sources of Power*

Answering God's Prayer

What if God spoke to you in an audible voice—if there was absolutely no doubt in your mind that it was Him and He was asking you to do something—would you hesitate even a moment in your obedience? What if I told you that He has already spoken to you in an audible voice and there is no doubt about what He wants you to do—but you didn't hear Him? God has spoken—and written—some very specific instructions to us. We can find them in the Holy Scriptures... but sometimes we can be selective in our hearing and remembering, and overlook some simple yet important commands.

I've often said things to my daughters that they didn't take to heart—and the consequences to them were unpleasant. I was hurt as well—it is painful for a father to know that his words have been heard by ears, but not heeded by hearts.

My three daughters love me very much, and my approval means the world to them. (By the way, their approval also means the world to me!) When I'm home, they'll often go out of their way to do the little things that melt my heart. They become little angels with their adoring faces and sweet voices... until one of their siblings annoys them. Then they undergo a brief but startling transformation: the same little angel whose eyes were gazing up at me in adoration can turn in an instant, directing a hateful glare and hurtful words at one of her siblings. Then they slip back into "angel" mode the very next moment, as if nothing had happened.

I have no doubt that my girls want nothing more than to make me happy. They know how to make me smile. But so often, they fail to do the one thing that they KNOW they should have done, something I've asked of them countless times: "Be nice to your sister!" My loving, passionate pleas fall on deaf ears when I see them hurting each other that way. Their behavior towards me could be flawless—but I'm not just looking at how they treat me, I'm also looking at how they treat each other.

My girls discovered an unpleasant physical reality: they cannot all be in close proximity to me without also being in close proximity to each other. *The closer they want to get to me, the closer they will be to each other...* and the more likely they are to annoy and respond to each other.

This behavior disappoints me deeply as an earthly father. It doesn't capture my heart... it doesn't impress me at all. The older my children get, the less tolerance I have for that sort of thing. I can't help but wonder how it makes our heavenly Father feel when His 'grown children' exhibit that same lack of maturity.... I've watched as people who appeared to have a deep encounter with God at the altar get up and can't even walk out the church door without making some disparaging comment about a fellow believer. I've listened as people who thought they were acting so "spiritual" complained that brothers and sisters in the Lord were bothering them during service. I'll hear them say things like:

"When so-and-so does such-and-such, it just breaks the atmosphere for me," or "I can't believe they let that person on the worship team," or "Why don't the 'big names' ever pray for me?" I'm sure this type of attitude doesn't impress God very much.

Five times in Scripture, Jesus prays that His disciples would be one. It is the only unanswered prayer that He ever prayed. He never had to pray more than a few words to heal the sick or even raise the dead, and never had to repeat His prayers before they became effective. But five times in John 17, Jesus prayed a prayer that has yet to be answered...that they may be one!

We have the power to answer His prayer. God wants you, and me, and each of His children to come closer to Him, and in so doing, to come closer together around His throne. What does He want you to do with your life? How can you have a closer walk with Him?

Why not start by cultivating a passion for what God is passionate about...His children, your brothers and sisters, the world around you! He wants you walking in unity with Him and His people.

That's what God wants from us—it is clear and undeniable, and when we choose to ignore it we break His heart. How can we keep coming to the altar, crying out "Lord, show me Your will for my life!" when we haven't even attempted to do what He has already so clearly revealed to us? Do we really think that impresses God? Jesus audibly spoke it when He prayed for unity in His body and saw to it that it was included in the Scriptures. There's your audible voice and written directions! What more could you want?

GodChasers.network newsletter

God Has Never Been Impressed by Buildings

For some reason the Christian world has forgotten that God has never been impressed by buildings. Pastors and members who meet in simple or makeshift structures constantly battle for earthly recognition as a legitimate church in town. Probably some of the multimillion dollar, splendorous church complexes in that same town *battle* for heavenly recognition as a legitimate church. Our attachment to steeples and stained glass *can* get in the way of real worship. If given a choice, God prefers passion over palace! If you recall, David wanted to construct a temple, but God told him He wasn't interested. If you look closely at the Bible passages describing the dedication of Solomon's huge temple, you will see God saying such things as,

> *But if you or your sons at all turn from following Me...then I will cut off Israel from the land which I have given them; and* **this house** *which I have consecrated for My name I* **will cast out of My sight**. *Israel will be a proverb and a byword among all peoples. And as for* **this house**, *which is exalted,* **everyone who passes by** [the ruins of] *it will be astonished and will hiss...*(1 Kings 9:6-8a).

When Jesus' disciples remarked about the magnificent beauty of Herod's temple in Jerusalem, He prophesied, "These things which you see—the days will come in which not one stone shall be left upon another that shall not be thrown down"—(Lk. 21:6). Yet God never said such things about David's tabernacle. In fact, He says just the opposite. He seems to be not saying, "*thrown down*," but rather, "Can I help you *prop up* your tent poles once again? Can I help restore what time has stolen and what the weakness of man has allowed to collapse? I want to preserve this house—the memories of 'man-encounters' here mean much to Me."

We want God encounters but God wants man encounters, because encounters with His children affect Him. He will "rip veils" and interrupt time to visit with His kids. When I put my schedule aside to "have tea" on the floor or in the playhouse with Andrea, it makes vivid memories for her; yet it also makes treasured memories for me!

Tommy Tenney – *God's Favorite House*

Forgiveness Is More Important for Us Than for "Them"

We need to forgive whether we feel we have a "right" to be angry or not. It is actually more important for us than it is for "them" because forgiveness keeps our hearts "clean" and it pleases God. If anyone in the Old Testament had a "right" to be angry with other people, it was Joseph. His jealous older brothers plotted to kill him, but decided to sell him into slavery instead. He worked as a slave to Pharaoh's head guard in Egypt, then he ended up in Pharaoh's prison after being falsely accused. Joseph refused to dwell on his "rights" or his "wrongs," and instead chose to forgive. This qualified him for God's favor and blessing and he was elevated to the number two position in Egypt as ruler under Pharaoh at the age of 30.

When Joseph finally met his brothers again, he had every "right" to be bitter and resentful (if there is such a thing). They had mistreated him and deceived their father, and Joseph had the power to order them killed on the spot. Instead, Joseph *chose* to forgive them and he became a savior to his entire family. When he saw his brothers, he couldn't control himself. He wept so loudly that the whole household of Pharaoh heard him. The world needs to know that "the community of the changed" know how to forgive. The lost and hurting around us need to know there is abundant forgiveness in the house and family of God.

God intends for our forgiveness to literally preserve and protect the lives of those who misuse or abuse us until they can turn their hearts to Him. Joseph's brothers were overcome with guilt and he begged them to forgive themselves. He said:

> But now, do not therefore be grieved or angry with your-selves because you sold me here; for God sent me before you to preserve life....And God sent me before you to preserve a posterity for you in the earth, and to save your lives by a great deliverance (Genesis 45:5,7).

This is the character of God! It is higher than any "right" we could ever have. Joseph never gave any evidence that he was bitter over his mistreatment by his brothers. He lived *a lifestyle of forgiveness.*

Sometimes we think we have forgiven someone when the truth is that we have reserved a special little room, a hidden closet of bit-terness, buried deep in our heart that we hope God never visits. We keep the person who offended us locked up in that secret place. When we are alone, we indulge ourselves by remembering "what they did to us ten years ago." Then we mentally pull out the offend-er and "beat up on them" for a while.

We like to say, "Oh, that's under the blood," but it isn't. The devil likes to hide in our secret rooms inhabited by an unforgiving spirit, but no devil or demon in hell can withstand forgiveness. The "prisoner" in our hearts has to be released. We must forgive and release the power of God in our lives.

The people of Jerusalem played the game of "now you are for-given, now you are not" with disastrous results during the life and ministry of Jeremiah the prophet. King Zedekiah had imprisoned Jeremiah for prophesying the fall of Jerusalem to Babylon when they were surrounded by the armies of King Nebuchadnezzar of Babylon and his allies. They faced impossible odds with no way of escape, but God had a plan that still applies to His people today.

After Jeremiah prophesied to King Zedekiah that the city would fall but he would live, the king decided to observe the "law of remis-sion." He called together the people of Jerusalem and they made a covenant to free all of their fellow Jews who were bond servants in their homes. They forgave every debt owed by their brethren and set them free, even though the debts weren't fully paid.

T.F. Tenney and Tommy Tenney – *Secret Sources of Power*

Be Prepared to Give Someone Your Yesterday Today

Sometimes we go through things not so much for us but for the sake of someone else. *Your yesterday may be someone else's today.* God may be preparing you to feed their today out of your experiences of yesterday. That doesn't mean you won't wonder why such things are happening to you at the time.

Hindsight is an invaluable way to learn how things fit into God's plan. There is no such thing as "waste" in God's economy. He knows exactly what He is doing. God led Moses the prince of Egypt and murderer into the desert to teach him how to be a shepherd and deliverer. It was in the "desert of relinquishment" that Moses learned many of the things he needed to lead Israel through the Sinai. Moses wasn't thrilled about going back to Egypt and all of its memories. He wanted to have a pity party but no one showed up but the devil. (That is what usually happens at pity parties.)

David was also familiar with the process of relinquishment. He was the one who wrote, "Yea, though I walk through the valley of the shadow of death..." (Ps. 23:4). Each one of us will experience our own valleys and feel the cold shadow of death on our shoulders at times. David, the same man who lived in a cave as an exile and outlaw, and later ran for his life when his own son plotted to kill him, has some words of wisdom for us.

The Psalmist who endured decades of "relinquishment" while running from Saul's armies said, "If you are in the valley of the shadow, just keep walking. What you need is an uninterrupted walk with God, even if He takes you through the dark valley. Just don't wallow in it. Don't linger there. Don't pitch your tent under that shadow. Above all, don't throw a pity party in that valley."

Moses discovered that the process of relinquishment could transform his strengths into weaknesses and his weaknesses into strengths. When Moses turned aside to investigate the burning bush on Mount Sinai, God called out to him from the bush and Moses said, "Here am I" (Ex. 3:4b KJV). Only seven verses later, Moses was saying, "Who am I...?" (Ex. 3:11b)

You will never find out who you are until you say to God, "Here I am." We must offer ourselves first. It is no good trying to find out what God wants *first*, and then deciding whether or not we are willing. We must offer ourselves unconditionally and simply say, "Here I am." This is what it means to relinquish ourselves to Him, and this is what releases the *power* of God in our lives.

God was patient with His reluctant deliverer. Moses didn't start by parting the Red Sea. He had to begin by taking small, tentative steps of faith to relinquish his fears and take hold of God's ability. "Moses, what is in your hand?" God asked. We know it was just a rod, a shepherd's staff, a mere stick. Yet that stick became a miracle *when Moses turned it loose* at God's command. When did it cease to be a miracle? The miraculous stopped and the mundane began when Moses picked it back up. *That is the power of relinquishment.*

It was customary for a shepherd in the time of Moses and David to whittle and carve his stories or personal history into the beam of his staff. Then it was passed from generation to generation as a family heirloom. When God said to Moses, "Give me your staff," it was as if He was saying, "*Give me your past.*" It was the last symbol of authority.

Moses left his scepter in Egypt. By then, the staff was the symbol of his authority over those bleating sheep. God was now saying, "Give Me your authority! Throw that down, too." Moses could have said, "You've already taken everything from me. I need this staff to lean on," but he chose to relinquish his past and embrace the will of God.

The Lord says to each of us, "Turn it loose if you want to be what I want you to be." It is in those moments that we discover the power of relinquishment. Only when everything and everyone but God is gone do we realize that God is enough.

T.F. Tenney and Tommy Tenney – *Secret Sources of Power*

If You Build It, He Will...

n the Old Testament, the Hebrew word translated as "glory" is *kabod*. It literally means weightiness or weighty splendor (James Strong, *Strong's Exhaustive Concordance of the Bible* [Peabody, MA: Hendrickson Publishers, n.d.], **glory** [#H3519, #H3513]). *I wonder how many times the "weighty glory" of God has visited us but not come in?* How often does He stand at the back door of our assemblies with His glory still hidden by His "hat and coat" while He scans the room?

We stop to count our spiritual goose bumps because we feel a cool breeze enter the room when the heavenly door opens. We tell one another, "Oh, God is here! He's visiting us again." Our singers rejoice and the band picks up the pace, but all too quickly it escapes us because we don't have what He is looking for. Most who have experienced visitations ask the question, "Why won't He stay? We begged Him to stay. Why can't we keep these moments?"

The answer is very simple: *We haven't built a mercy seat to hold the glory of God.* There is no place for Him to sit! What is comfortable to you and I is not comfortable to the *kabod*, the weightiness of God. We are happy to sit in our comfortable spiritual recliners all day, but the seat of God, the mercy seat, is a little different. It is the only seat on earth that can bear the weight of His glory and compel Him to come in and *stay*.

God is looking for a church that has learned how to build a mercy seat for His glory. When He finds a house that has paid the price to build Him a resting place, He will come and He will stay.

That is when we will see a revival that is unlike any we have ever seen before. I am convinced that we don't even have a word for it. This kind of revival can only come when God comes in His weighty glory and takes His seat of honor in His house—to stay.

We must learn how to build a mercy seat. I remember the line from a motion picture I saw during a transoceanic flight that greatly affected me the first time I saw it. The motion picture was *The Field of Dreams*, and the line that came to mind in that instant was, "If you build it, *He* will come...," a lesson David learned.

The southern region of the United States is generally recognized for its "southern hospitality." Since I'm a southern boy, I thought I understood some of the basic principles of hospitality. I felt that way until God sent me, unasked, on a journey that led me to invest about 30 percent of my ministry among the Chinese that year. (I still minister quite often in mainland China and Taiwan.) He said, "I'm going to show you something about honor that most westerners do not know."

I learned that Oriental people have an ability to give honor that surpasses anything I have ever witnessed anywhere else. We practice hospitality in the West, but we are kind of casual about it: "Oh, hi. Come in. Sit down if you want to."

It is not that way with the Chinese. They are very careful to focus all their attention and energies on their guests. They put their guests' well-being first, and they work tirelessly to put their guests' comfort, peace, and happiness above their own. The way the Chinese carefully prepare in advance for their guests' arrival is an open statement declaring that those guests are highly valued and respected. They even carefully reserve the traditional seat of honor...the chair furthest from and facing the door.

Tommy Tenney – *God's Favorite House*

David's Long Sweaty Journey Versus No-Sweat Revival

hristians around the world are saying, "We want revival; we want a move of God." Unfortunately, we haven't learned from David's mistakes. Often we try to do the same thing he did the first time he attempted to bring God's presence to Jerusalem. We cram the holy things of God on a new cart of man's making, thinking God will be pleased. Then we are shocked when we discover His disdain! He won't let oxen pull on carts carrying His glory! We expect somebody or something else to "sweat" out the hard part of revival. All we want to do is sing and dance in the procession. These half-baked, man-centered revival celebrations go as smoothly as David's first "ark party"—until we hit a God-bump at Nachon's threshing floor.

These "speed" bumps on the road to revival may well be the hand of God saying,

"No more of that! I will let you handle Me casually and cavalierly only so long. I will only let you handle Me with no sweat up to a certain point. However, if you really want to move Me from 'Heaven to earth,' you are going to 'sweat' it out. Don't try to transport My glory on your rickety man-made programs, methods, and agendas. You can have your cart or My ark—but not both!"

David retreated and did some research after Uzzah was struck dead at Nachon's threshing floor. *Uzzah died after he tried to stabilize what God had shaken.* We still insist on smoothing out the bumps and rounding off the edges of God's commandment. We are futilely trying to create an "Uzzah-friendly" environment when we prize man's comfort above God's comfort. I often put it this way: "*Seeker-friendly is fine, but Spirit-friendly is fire!*"

David discovered that God had told Moses that the ark should be transported only on the shoulders of sanctified Levites. God had had enough of man's ways, and He rocked the cart to let David's crew know about it. He didn't want anyone holding up what He was striking down.

Why would David put the ark on a cart in the first place? To the mind of man, it was logical to put a heavy box on a cart for such a long journey. Besides, that is how the Philistines did it. The ark of the covenant was a box constructed of gopher wood and overlaid with gold inside and out. It measured about four feet long, two-and-a-half feet wide, and two-and-a-half feet deep. The ark also had a gold top with two solid-gold cherubim mounted on it, and it was carried with gold-overlaid poles run through solid-gold rings attached to the side. Gold is one of the densest and heaviest materials on earth. Can you imagine how much the ark weighed? No wonder they attempted the journey on a cart! David learned the hard way that God doesn't think like men do. His ways—*and the road to a holy revival*—are higher and "sweatier."

Tommy Tenney – *God's Favorite House*

Real Revival Is When...

We don't understand revival; in fact, we don't even have the slightest concept of what true revival is. For generations we have thought of revival in terms of a banner across the road or over a church entryway. We think revival means a silver-tongued preacher, some good music, and a few folks who decide they're going to join the church. No! Real revival is when people are eating at a restaurant or walking through the mall when they suddenly begin to weep and turn to their friends and say, "I don't know what's wrong with me, but I know I've got to get right with God."

Real revival is when the most "difficult" and unreachable person you know comes to Jesus against all odds and possibilities. Frankly, the main reason such people aren't reached any other time is because they are seeing too little of God and too much of man. We've tried to cram doctrine down people's throats, and we've printed enough tracts to paper the walls of entire buildings. I thank God for every person reached by a gospel tract, but people don't want doctrine, they don't want tracts, and they don't want our feeble arguments; they just want Him! (When will we learn that if people can be argued into the faith, then they can just as easily be argued out of it as well?) People may be attracted by our great music for a while, but it will only keep them interested as long as the music is good. We must not compete with the world in areas where they are as competent (or better than) us. They can't compete with God's presence.

I can tell you a secret right now if you promise *to* tell someone else. Do you want to know when people will start coming inside the confines of your local church building? They will come as soon as they hear that the *presence of God* is in the place. It's time to rediscover the power of the manifest presence of God.

God is looking for enough hungry people to receive His presence. When He comes, you won't need any advertisements in the newspaper, or on radio or television. All you need is God, and people will come from far and near on any given night! I'm not talking about theory or fiction—it is already happening. It all begins with the prayer of the hungry:

There's got to be more...

Tommy Tenney – *The God Chasers*

False Premises About Revival and Anointing Produce Misunderstanding

ometimes we have false premises about revival and the people God uses in true revivals. These false premises about revival and the anointing can produce a lot of misunderstanding. Someone asked Duncan Campbell to define revival, and he touched on this in his reply:

"First let me tell you what I mean by revival. An evangelistic campaign or a special meeting is not revival. In a successful evangelistic campaign or crusade, there will be hundreds, even thousands of people making decisions for Jesus Christ, but the community may remain untouched, and the churches continue much the same as before the outreach.

"But in revival God moves in the region. Suddenly the community becomes God conscious, and the Spirit of God grips men and women in such a way that even work is given up as people give themselves to waiting upon God. In the midst of the Lewis Awakening [what we call the Hebrides revival], the parish minister...wrote, 'The Spirit of the Lord was resting wonderfully on the different townships of the region. His presence was in the homes of the people, on the meadow, and the moorland, and the public roads.'

"This presence of God is the supreme characteristic of a God-sent revival. Of the hundreds who found Jesus Christ during this time, fully 75 percent were saved before they came near a meeting, or heard a sermon by myself or any other minister in the parish. The power of God was moving in an operation that the fear of God gripped the souls of men before they ever reached the meetings."

I will never be content merely to see the glory of God flow down the beautiful carpeted aisles of our churches. I want to see it flow down Main Street in an uncontrollable, unstoppable flood of glory that carries along everything in its path. I want His glory to invade the malls, grocery stores, health spas, and bars across town. I want to hear unchurched people say that they had to abandon an expensive entrée at their favorite restaurant to follow the dripping trail of God's glory to a church somewhere and demand, "Somebody tell me what to do!"

If good sermons and good songs were going to save the world, it would already be saved. There's a missing ingredient, and that "Divine Ingredient" is knocking at the door. The Hebrides revival provides a brief hint of what happens when glory breaks out. While describing the first days of the movement in the Hebrides Islands, Duncan Campbell remembered closing out a service in a crowded church and noticing that the congregation seemed reluctant to disperse. Many of the people just stood outside of the church building in a silence that was almost tense.

"Suddenly a cry is heard within, a young man burdened for the souls of his fellow men is pouring out his soul in intercession." Campbell said the man prayed until he collapsed and lay prostrate on the floor of the church building. He said, "The congregation, moved by a power they could not resist, came back into the church, and a wave of conviction swept over the gathering, moving strong men to cry to God for mercy."

Tommy Tenney – *God's Favorite House*

David Fueled the Flame of God's Presence With 24-Hour Worship

How can we recreate or "compete" with the kind of worship God receives in Heaven? David instructed sanctified Levites to keep fueling the flame of God's presence with 24-hour worship every day. (Don't get into legalism and think, "I have to help my church set up a 24-hour prayer vigil." If God tells you and your church leadership to do it, then do it. If not, ask Him what He wants you to do and do it.)

Remember that you can beg for God to come all you want, but until you prepare a place where His weighty glory can safely dwell, He may visit but He cannot stay. I don't know about you, but I am tired of visits. Somehow we have to reclaim the ability to *host the Holy Ghost*. David knew how to do it.

David surrounded that ark with worshipers so that the glory of God would keep flickering. For the first time in history, Israelites, pagans, or heathen could stand near Mount Zion in Jerusalem and literally see the blue flame of God's glory flickering between the outstretched arms and dancing feet of the worshipers in David's tabernacle! How could this be? It was because David's tabernacle was a place marked by open-veiled and unfettered worship.

I often illustrate this concept of surrounding God with worship in public meetings by calling up three or more volunteers to join me in front of the audience or congregation. Almost every time one of the volunteers will step into position facing the audience because that is the way we have been conditioned. I'll tell the volunteer (for the benefit of the audience), "No, son, don't face the congregation or the choir. Stand right here and lift up your hands in a posture of worship toward the One on the throne."

(This may explain why the world can't see God when it looks at the Church—it sees only us. That is probably because we don't stand in the gap, and we prefer to face the world instead of God while performing our religious duties. There is too much of man in the church, and too little of God.) Facing man can only cause us to respond to man's approval. *For "mercy seat" worship, you must turn your back on man.* **Seek the face of God. Lose the fear of man— and gain the fear of God.**

David did more than surround the ark of God with sanctified worshipers. He made sure that their primary focus was to minister to God through praise, worship, and adoration. The Levites, the Old Testament ministers of worship and praise, stood between the world on the outside and the unveiled glory of God on the inside.

For the first time since His final walk with Adam and Eve in the garden of Eden, God found a house where there was no veil or dividing walls between His glory and the frail flesh of men. It wasn't needed because **the worshipers had become the veil** and protective walls as they surrounded God's glory with a covering cloud of repentant, sacrificial worship and praise. For lack of a better term, I call this precarious place between the porch of man and the altar of God "*the weeping zone.*" This is the miracle that made David's humble tent become God's favorite house.

Two key Scripture passages may help you understand why David managed to build a tabernacle without a veil or walls without seeing people die by the hundreds or thousands. First, God said, "And I sought for a man among them, that should make up the hedge, and stand in the gap before Me for the land, that I should not destroy it: but I found none." Secondly, John seems to describe the two components of God's glory when he wrote, "We beheld His glory...full of grace and truth."

Tommy Tenney – *God's Favorite House*

He Took Time Off for a Prayer Meeting

avid didn't have a nervous breakdown or take on the unnecessary weight of personal guilt over something he didn't cause and couldn't change. He said, "Give me the prayer shawl. Bring me that old ephod." He got under that prayer shawl and said to himself, "I've got to talk to God!" Can you imagine how that looked to his fighting men? In the midst of absolute chaos and emotional ruin, this man just shut down everything and went to prayer. Even though an unknown enemy appeared to be running off with everything he owned and every person he loved, David took time off for a prayer meeting. Did he know something we don't know?

Everything was stacked against David; the sounds of discontent and despair filled the air around him. Yet he thought, *I can't listen to this anymore. I have to get a sure word from the Lord Jehovah.* In a time of desperate crisis, David was distressed and hurt; but he didn't load up with sorrow, anger, and despair. *He unloaded.* He prayed until he got his word from the Lord. It was a simple instruction and promise, but it was enough: *"Pursue them. I am with you. You're not going to lose a thing. Here's the plan...."*

What if David didn't know when or how to unload? What would you do if you found yourself in David's situation? *Too often we panic when we ought to pray; we faint when we ought to "faith."* This isn't a matter of "faking" it—*it is a time to "**FAITH**" it!* This is the power that comes with unloading.

The enemy has no power to harm you in and of himself. He gets his power from *you* when you release it to him! However, when you unload your own preconceived notions of power and responsibility and give yourself to Christ, the Holy Spirit is released by you and through you.

What do you do when life shows up and God doesn't? You focus on Him anyway and unload the situation into His care. Peter, Jesus' most impetuous disciple, wrote in his later and more mature years, "[Cast] all your care upon Him, for He cares for you" (1 Pet. 5:7).

T.F. Tenney and Tommy Tenney – *Secret Sources of Power*

God Misses the Song of the Heart

od remembers when lucifer and the sons of the morning used to sing His praises with unearthly beauty and power. It *is as if* He says, "When will that be restored?" He is still surrounded by six-winged seraphim who unceasingly declare His glory, but He misses the song of the heart.

Despite years of research, *I cannot find a single place in the Bible where music is mentioned as a part of Heaven's environment after the fall of satan.* I have asked numerous theologians about this. Most people respond to my statement by saying, "Well, Tommy, you remember what the angels sang at the birth of Christ in Bethlehem, don't you? They sang, 'Glory to God in the highest, peace on earth, good will toward men.' "

At that point I have to gently direct them back to the biblical passages in the Gospels. "No, if you read it carefully, you will see that the Bible doesn't say they sang. I really hate to mess up all our wonderful Christmas plays and holiday hymns. It won't hurt a thing to let your little children dress up as little angels and sing in a Christmas cantata, so don't worry about it. I just want you to know what the Bible actually says":

*And suddenly there was with the angel a multitude of the heavenly host **praising** God, and **saying**, Glory to God in the highest, and on earth peace, good will toward men* (Luke 2:13-14).

Job 38:7 says, "When the morning stars *sang* together, and all the sons of God shouted for joy." The context clearly places this event at the very creation of our universe *just before lucifer's fall.* (See Isaiah

14:12-15.) After the fall, I can't find any literal Bible reference to singing
or music in Heaven. I don't have a problem with people who say, "Well,
I had a vision and heard angels singing"; I am just saying that I can't
find it mentioned in the Bible once satan was ejected from Heaven.

If music fell when satan fell, then that explains why the bulk of
the satanic influence in our world comes from the realm of music.
Music is his venue, so we shouldn't be surprised that the first place
problems often show up in most churches is in the area of music and
worship. Obviously, not all music "comes from satan," but he exerts
great influence through music. This also explains something else...

The Church spends countless hours crafting sermons, arranging
music scores, and rehearsing choirs and singers to make sure they are
just right. Yet no matter how much energy we spend pursuing excel-
lence in those areas, I must tell you we will never compete with the
world's symphony orchestras or the bands and artists featured on
MTV or VH1. In fact, we are not supposed to compete in those arenas!

Before you slam this book shut and toss it in the garbage can,
I want you to understand something:

**Our music may never be as good as the world's music
because our value system is different from the world's.**

*We are not after perfection so much
as we are after Presence.*

When the Church turns all its focus and energies toward the
technical and professional perfection of our well-rehearsed music,
our crafted sermons, and our tightly scripted services, we can
unknowingly begin competing in the wrong arena. We need to stick
with the one arena in which no one can compete with us—the art
and ability to pull down the manifest presence of God. *Technical perfection may win the praise of men, but only the anointing and glory of
God can melt their hardened hearts.*

At some point we've got to turn man's volume down and turn
God's volume up. A Damascus Road encounter will turn a murder-
er like Saul into a martyr named Paul in less than 30 seconds.
Perfected music won't do that, but *perfected praise* might attract
Him, and His presence will!

Tommy Tenney – *God's Favorite House*

God Is Raising Up His Own Worship Team!

When God ejected satan and his cohorts, He was also dismissing the angelic worship team. As always, God already had a plan for a better replacement team that reflected His wisdom and glory in ways no created being could ever fathom. He would raise up a team of worshipers who would praise Him freely while wearing the linen white choir robes of the redeemed sprinkled with the crimson blood of their Redeemer!

Isn't it sad that in church we often quarrel over *the one thing that means the most to God?* Once again, we are talking about worship. He loves worship. It is the one thing that attracts Him to our gathering more than anything else. When God wanted to hear a song early in the first century, He had to invade a Philippian jail to hear two beaten preachers croak it out. He got so excited He patted His foot and triggered a massive earthquake! (See Acts 16:23-26.)

If God wants to hear a song today, *He comes to church.* We can't afford to allow the corruption that removed worship from Heaven to get into our worship today! Satan knows this, so he will do anything he can to distract us from worship and incite us to criticize and divide. The Gospels tell the story of a man at Gadara with a legion of devils who immediately came to Jesus when His anointed foot touched the shore of that region. He had never seen or heard about Jesus, yet "something" drew him to the Master.

When he saw Jesus "from afar," he *ran* to meet the Lord so quickly that he met Jesus "immediately" after He landed! This man had approximately two thousand demons frantically clawing at his soul to keep him from responding to Jesus' presence. (There were at least enough demons to possess and destroy two thousand pigs. Who knows, some of those pigs may have had "double occupancy.") (See Mark 5:1-13.)

This demoniac was desperate for Jesus. He probably ran at least a mile to reach Jesus, and even though this man was full of frightened, desperate demons, he still managed to kneel down and worship Jesus! If two thousand demons couldn't keep a man from worshiping Jesus, how can we justify allowing so many unimportant things to keep *us* from worshiping Him?

T.F. Tenney and Tommy Tenney – *Secret Sources of Power*

Ye Have Not Because...

Compared to what God *wants to do*, we're digging for crumbs in the carpet when He has hot loaves baking in the ovens of Heaven! He is not the God of crumbs and lack. He is waiting just to dispense unending loaves of His life-giving presence, but our problem was described long ago by James the apostle, "...ye have not, because ye ask not" (Jas. 4:2 KJV). Yet the psalmist David sings through the tunnel of time that "his seed" never go "begging for bread" (see Ps. 37:25).

We need to understand that what we have, where we are, and what we are doing is *small* compared to what He wants to do among and through us. Young Samuel was a prophet in a generation of transition much like ours. The Bible tells us that early in Samuel's life, "...the word of the Lord was precious in those days; there was no open vision" (1 Sam. 3:1).

One night Eli the old high priest went to bed, and by that point in his life his eyesight had grown so poor that he could barely see anything. Part of our problem in the historical Church is that our eyesight has grown dim and we can't see like we should. We've become satisfied with church proceeding in the dim "normal and status quo" mode. We just keep going through the motions, lighting the lamps and shuffling from dusty room to dusty room as if God was still speaking to us. But when He really does speak, we think people are dreaming. When He really does appear, dim eyes can't see Him. When He really does move, we are reluctant to accept it for fear we will "bump into something unfamiliar" in our dim, lamp-less darkness. It frustrates us when God "moves the furniture" on us. We tell the young Samuels among us, "Go back to sleep. Just keep doing things the way I've taught you to do them, Samuel. It's okay. It has always been this way."

No, it hasn't always been that way! And I'm not happy with it being that way—*I want more!* I don't know about you, but every empty seat I see in a church building screams out to me, "I could be filled with some former citizen of Moab! Can't you put a body in this seat?" I don't know about you, but that just feeds my holy frustration, my divine discontent.

> And [before] **the lamp of God went out in the temple** of the Lord, where the ark of God was, and Samuel was laid down to sleep;
>
> That the Lord called Samuel: and he answered, Here am I (1 Samuel 3:3-4 KJV).

The lamp of God was flickering low and was just about to go out, but that didn't disturb Eli. (He lived in a permanent state of semi-darkness.) Young Samuel, though, said, "I hear something." It is time for us to admit that the lamp of God is flickering. Yes, it is still burning, but things are not as they should be. We look at this little flickering lamp casting low light in the Church here and there and say, "Oh, it's revival!" It may be for the handful who can get close enough to see it, but what about those who are at a distance? What about the lost who never read our magazines, watch our TV shows, or listen to the latest Christian teaching tapes? We need the light of the glory of God bright enough to be seen from a distance. In other words, it is time for the glory of God, the lamp of God, to break out of the Church "bushel" to illuminate our cities! (See Matthew 5:15.)

I believe that God is about to release the "spirit of a breaker" (see Mic. 2:13) to come and literally break the heavens open so that everybody can eat and feed at God's table. Before the heavens can open, though, the fountains of the deep must be broken. (See Genesis 1:8; 7:11.) It's time for some church, somewhere, to forget about trying to be a "politically correct church" and break open the heavens that the manna might fall and start feeding the spiritually hungry of the city! It's time that we punch a hole in the heavens and break through in hungry travail so the glory of God can begin to shine down on our city. But we can't even get a trickle to flow down the aisle, much less see His glory flow through the streets, *because we're not really hungry.* We are like the Laodiceans, full and content.

Father, I pray that a spirit of spiritual violence will grip our hearts, that You will turn us into warriors of worship. I pray that we will not stop until we break through the heavens, until there's a crack in the heavenlies, until there is an open heaven. Our cities and nation need You, Lord. We need You. We're tired of digging through the carpet for crumbs. Send us Your hot bread from Heaven, send us the manna of Your presence....

No matter what you need or feel you lack in your life—what you *really* need is *Him.* And the way to get Him is to get hungry. I pray that God will give you an impartation of *hunger* because that will qualify you for the promise of the fullness. Jesus said: "Blessed are they which do hunger and thirst after righteousness: for they shall be filled" (Mt. 5:6).

If we can get hungry, then He can make us holy. Then He can put the pieces of our broken lives back together. But our hunger is the key. So when you find yourself digging for crumbs in the carpet at the House of Bread, you should be praying, "Lord, stir up a firestorm of hunger in me."

Tommy Tenney – *The God Chasers*

Follow Him to the Weeping Zone for the Lost

*J*esus Christ did a finished work on the cross, and He extends the free gift of life to everyone. Our "ministry of reconciliation" involves taking up His cross daily and following Him into the weeping zone for the lost. When repentant, bloody-handed, sacrificing worshipers take their place between the unredeemed and the consuming glory of God, an interesting thing happens.

We know from the Scriptures that judgment begins and ends at the house of God. (See 1 Peter 4:17.)When God's people become worshipers and stand in the gap, *they "filter" the truth and judgment component of glory.* That means that the only component of God's glory that rushes past them to flow in the streets of the city is grace and mercy. This is reminiscent of David's day, when anyone and everyone could look at the *shekinah* glory of God and live because they were peering at the mercy seat between the covering filter of the outstretched arms of worshipers.

Our cities don't need better sermons or better songs. They need "gap people" who can reach for God with one hand and for the world with the other. Are you called to take a stand in the weeping zone? Can you forget what man says while reaching out to God with one hand in repentant, broken worship and reaching out to unredeemed man with the other? With that hand extended, you declare: "I am going to open the heavens and keep them propped open until revival sweeps through my city!" Like the intercessors of old, we must cry, "If You are going to kill them, then kill me. If You don't send revival to my nation, just kill me. Give me spiritual children, or I die." (See Exodus 32; Genesis 30:1.)

Do you really want revival? *Build a mercy seat for God.* Prepare something that is so desirable and attractive to God that He can't resist joining you and the worshipers. Allow Him to build again the tabernacle of David in your midst. Surround Him with worship and adoration if you want to entice Him to come and stay with you. *Build a mercy seat!*

Can you imagine what would happen if He left His throne in Heaven to come sit with us in a mercy seat composed of our praise and worship? There is a reason the world can't see Him as He is. *We have never built a place for Him to sit.* Foxes have holes and birds have nests, but the glory of God has no place to sit—no earthly mercy seat! Of course our furniture is simple by Heaven's standards, and we could never pass for six-winged seraphim. How can earthly worship match heavenly worship? I don't know, but I do know it doesn't take much! Jesus said, "If I can just get two or three of you to agree, I'll come in—not to the side, but in the middle of them." (See Matthew 18:20.) Why? Because God dwells in the middle of the worship.

If you want the manifested presence of God to break out in your church and city, then remember that He probably won't come to me alone, nor to you alone. His first choice and His promise is that He will come *in the middle* of us as we worship Him according to the heavenly pattern.

If you build it, He will come!

"Father, You said that out of the mouth of babes and suck-lings You have perfected praise. We admit that our best is pitiful praise, that it cannot match the heavenly vision, that it cannot reach the heights of perfection we understand is in Heaven.

"Nevertheless, according to the heavenly pattern, we delight in surrounding You with repentant worship. Rebuild Your beloved tabernacle of David in our hearts, dear Lord. Yes, we will worship You with all our hearts. Yes, with joy we will bow down before You as our Lord and King.

"We call for Your manifested presence to fill this place, Father. We ask You to fill this city, to fill this nation, to fill this world until the whole earth is covered with Your glory, O God, like the waters cover the sea. Come sit in our midst on Your mercy seat!"

Tommy Tenney – *God's Favorite House*

Jesus' Prayer of Forgiveness Unleashed the Power of God

esus' words and deeds on the cross unleashed God's supernatural power of forgiveness and set in motion a divine sequence of events:

1. *He forgave all of our trespasses or debts.* He also taught us to pray, "Forgive us our debts, as we forgive our debtors" (Mt. 6:12). A debt is something legally owed. Perhaps someone legally and rightfully owes you an apology, but it is a debt they will not pay. What do you do? Forgive them anyway.

2. *He canceled out our decree of death* when He wiped out the laws and regulations we could never keep, and the mountain of sins we accumulated. Then He took the whole document of rules, the list of our failures, and the certificate of death and nailed it to the cross as something to be crucified and buried. If people don't respond to your forgiveness, it becomes their problem, not yours. Offer it anyway. Sometimes you have to settle for the proverbial "fifty cents on the dollar" in matters like this. You are responsible for your half of the settlement—the *forgiving* and *canceling* part.

3. *He disarmed the principalities and powers* when He forgave our debts and sins. Forgiveness tore up hell's playground, and your forgiveness of others destroys the best-laid plans of the enemy meant for their destruction.

Do you want God's power in your life? It comes with the power of forgiveness. *When you forgive you cancel the debt and evict the devil.* How can we make the claim this "evicts the devil"? We aren't claiming the enemy can "have" you, but the Bible makes it clear there are ways he can legally claim the right to "hitch a ride" and harass you if there is resentment or unforgiveness in your life.

Jesus said in one place, *"The ruler of this world is coming, and **he has nothing in Me**"* (Jn. 14:30b). Satan lives in darkness and he cannot bear the light of God's glory. He persistently works to get one little shaft of darkness into your heart in the form of resentment, unforgiveness, or a spirit of bitterness toward someone else. The apostle Paul said,

> *"Be angry, and do not sin": do not let the sun go down on your wrath, **nor give place to the devil*** (Ephesians 4:26-27).

> *Now whom you forgive anything, I also forgive. For if indeed I have forgiven anything, I have forgiven that one for your sakes in the presence of Christ, **lest satan should take advantage of us; for we are not ignorant of his devices*** (2 Corinthians 2:10-11).

Unforgiveness in any form gives satan a comfortable "place" of darkness that becomes a legal handle or handgrip on your life from which he can take advantage of you and make your life miserable. (The darkness of sin doesn't belong to God; it is part of satan's realm. It gives satan "stock" in your life, so he can rightfully show up at your "stockholder meetings" and wreak havoc.) However, the enemy lives in darkness. As long as you are full of the light of God's presence without the darkness of unforgiveness, that light has the power to totally dispel and repel satan from every area of your life.

Any discussion concerning the devil and his kingdom should be conducted from the perspective of our new position in Christ. In the Book of Ephesians, we are told that God *"raised us up together, and made us sit together in the heavenly places in Christ Jesus"* (Eph. 2:6).

The devil's principalities and powers are not "looking down on us"; we are looking down on them from our spiritual position in Christ, seated in heavenly places. The forces of darkness are *beneath* us because they are bound by the power of the blood of the Lamb, the name of Jesus, the Word of God, and the power of forgiveness.

T.F. Tenney and Tommy Tenney – *Secret Sources of Power*

Jesus Said, "I Think I Found One..."

o you know what God eats when He's hungry? *Worship.* Do you remember the woman at the well? When Jesus told her about His living water and said that His Father was seeking true worshipers, she gave the answer He was looking for. She said, "I want that water." In that moment Jesus might have mused, *I think I found one. That is what I was waiting for.*

When the disciples came back, they said, "Lord, we've got Your Burger King for You," or "Here's Your McDonalds Big Mac, Master." They were shocked when He said, "I'm not hungry. I've had meat to eat you don't know of." It was as if He were thinking, *You wouldn't understand it, but I've been receiving worship from a rejected woman at the well. I've done My Father's will and found a worshiper. After that feast, I don't need anything you have for Me.* (See John 4:31-34.)

God comes to earth because His growling hunger pains for worship draw Him to the imperfect praise of His children, who say, "*I luv You, Daddy.*" He isn't particularly impressed with our polished singing and multimillion dollar buildings. It is all pitiful by celestial standards, but it is precious to Him because He loves us.

> "Red and yellow, black and white,
> They are precious in His sight.
> Jesus loves the *little children* of the world."

He comes because we hold up childlike imperfect praise with hearts full of love—like a child reaching up and a Father reaching down.

He is out to populate Heaven with worshipers who can fulfill that missing part that has been absent ever since lucifer fell. Jesus auditioned the woman at the well in search of that "high note" of transparency and purity. He gave her the opportunity to answer a question for which He already knew the answer: *Can you hit this note?* He wondered, as He searched under the "rock of the human will" for a worshiper. Then He told the woman, "Go get your husband." She could have hidden her sin or covered her broken life with the fig leaves of a lie, but for once in her life she thought, *No, I know it's not very pretty, but I'm going to tell Him the truth.* Then she said, "I have no husband."

Jesus could no longer contain His excitement, and He interrupted her to say, "You have well said, 'I have no husband,' for you have had five husbands, and the one whom you now have is not your husband; in that you spoke truly" (Jn. 4:17b-18).

This was the high note of transparency and purity He was looking for. Now He had something He could work with. He began to talk to her about the living water. By the time He was done, she was ready to abandon her waterpots at the well. She ran back to the village to tell the people she had previously avoided all about the incredible Man at the well. She was so transformed that the same woman whom whole the village had rejected now led them back to Jacob's well to meet the Source of living water. *One conversation with the Master brought credibility to her—she had one worship encounter with Him, and the whole village listened.*

Tommy Tenney – *God's Favorite House*

Don't Fight With Your Tongue, Fight on Your Knees

Whether we like the terminology or not, these are "battle tactics." The simple truth about "spiritual warfare" is that most of the battles we try to fight with our tongues are better fought on our knees. The greatest battles are waged in the heavenlies, and by definition, *spiritual warfare* is a *spiritual* thing that must be won in the *spirit realm.* As for the tongue, it is like a double-edged sword. It may not weigh much, but very few people can hold it (including most Christians). We usually end up doing more damage than good once our tongues get going.

Even though satan is a loser whose entire existence has been corrupted by pride, he still has enough traces of angelic beauty, light, and intelligence to transform himself into an angel of light when necessary. (See 2 Corinthians 11:14.) He is both brilliantly stupid and seductively beautiful, and this combination of traits makes satan especially dangerous to the uninformed, "partially-knowledgeable" Christian. Satan still knows how angels are supposed to operate and often he can fool those who have failed to "rightly divide the word of truth" (See 2 Tim. 2:15).

Some people wonder why satan doesn't show up more often in the Old Testament. By one count, satan or Lucifer appears only 15 times in just four of the 39 books of the Old Testament, yet the four Gospels alone mention satan, the devil, or evil spirits at least 61 times. Why? When Jesus the light of the world arrived, His piercing light illuminated the darkness and exposed the old serpent for what he was. The Lord planted the Church on a hill to be the light of the world after His resurrection, and commanded us to do what He did: to expose and destroy the works of satan.

The devil can be very deceptive. We know he can *appear* to be an angel of light. It is almost guaranteed he will *not* show up in a red suit with horns and a pitchfork. It would be too easy for us to recognize him. He prefers to approach us in various disguises. Our love for "stereotypes and assumptions" about the enemy is another weakness he uses against us.

Many Christians are fooled when they assume satan only shows up in seedy bars, crack shacks, or houses of ill repute. Actually, he already "owns" those places, so they don't require his personal attention. He is more likely to be often found hiding behind the pews in God's house near folks who have "just the right atmosphere" of rebellion, jealousy, resentment, or unforgiveness in their hearts. He doesn't own that house yet, but he has been after the property since time began.

Satan has a special ability to infiltrate areas of beauty and creativity such as the visual arts, music, and literature. Satan is not creative because he lost all creativity the day his relationship with the God of creation (and creativity) was severed. However, he can still recognize creativity in the human race, and *he is quick to add demonic power to human ability*—for the price of a soul and the right to corrupt it for his purposes. That is why some of the material labeled as "quality literature" today is nothing more than X-rated pornographic reading.

The enemy is just clever enough to help gullible humans phrase their twisted thoughts to fit the minimum criteria for "art." He knows how to mix sensuous body language, alluring beat, and X-rated lyrics to entice the human heart and win every award the world has to offer! It is sad but true: We are easily lured by the beauty and deceived by the power behind the throne.

T.F. Tenney and Tommy Tenney – *Secret Sources of Power*

Who Will Find the Ancient Keys That Jingled in God's Hand?

The thing God promised is going to happen, and a flood of God's glory is going to come. It is going to start somewhere with someone, but where? Who will find the ancient keys that jingled in the hands of God when He told Peter, "Here are the keys to the Kingdom. Whatever you open on earth will be opened in Heaven"? (See Matthew 16:19). Who will hear a knock at the other side and slip that ancient key into that door to open the gate of Heaven? Wherever it happens, whoever opens that door, the result will be an unstoppable, immeasurable flood of the glory of God. If the glory of God is going to cover the earth, it has to start somewhere. Why not here? Why not you?

There are some Kingdom keys lying around, and somebody has to find them and prop the door open. God said, "I sought for a man among them who would make a wall, and stand in the gap before Me on behalf of the land, that I should not destroy it; but I found no one" (Ezek. 22:30). We need to strip away our overly religious ways of looking at things to really understand what God is saying. Where and what is this "gap" that God wants us to fill?

On one occasion, I took my entire family to Atlanta, Georgia, so they could be with me while I spoke at a church in that city. When departure time came, everyone filed out of the hotel room and headed for the elevator. Everyone had their hands full of bags, suitcases, and packages, including my youngest daughter. It seems like she has her own little family of stuffed animal figures called "Beanie Babies," and on this occasion she had brought the entire "family" along in her overstuffed backpack.

Have you ever seen little children trying to carry more than they can handle? Andrea was dragging her backpack down the hallway and lagging behind a little bit. The elevator in that particular hotel closed really quickly, and just as Andrea began to step onto the elevator, the door started closing on her. Everyone else was already on the elevator.

Andrea instinctively backed out of the elevator as quickly as she could, and that was when I saw a look of panic flood her face. I could imagine what was going through her mind in that moment: *Dear God, they are going to leave me here! I'll be stuck up here all by myself in this hotel while they drive away without me.*

My fatherly instincts also kicked in when the door started to close. I quickly thrust my hand between the elevator doors and hoped I would be able to force them back open. I finally got it open, but I literally had to force my hands between the doors and physically push them apart. Once I pried open the doors, I stepped between them and held them open. In that moment, I saw a look of sheer relief on Andrea's face, and she said, "My Daddy is ho'ding it open for me." With a sheepish grin and a little girl giggle, she snuck in between those doors and felt safe once again.

God never intended for us to use our favorite hymns or worship songs to mark our divine encounters or to hold open the gates of Heaven. A sermon won't do it; nor will a sparkling personality or a powerful healing ministry do it. God has a better idea. *Prop open that gate with your own life!* Become a doorkeeper and open the door to let the light of Heaven shine on your church and city.

Tommy Tenney – *God's Favorite House*

David Entertained God's Presence Continually for 36 Years!

avid discovered a key that we need to rediscover in our day. He did more than return God's presence to Jerusalem. He did more than display God's glory in an open tent without walls or a veil of separation. Somehow he managed to *entertain God's presence in his humble tent and keep an open heaven over all Israel for almost 36 years!* David's generation benefited from his worship.

When we open the windows of Heaven through our worship, we also need to post a guard—a doorkeeper—inside the dimension of God (worship) to hold open the windows of Heaven. In David's day, the Levitical worshipers surrounded the ark of the covenant with continuous worship and praise. *They enjoyed the benefits of a continuously open heaven because somebody stood in the gate and held it open.* If you are a pastor or church leader, your primary responsibility in your city is to be a gatekeeper. You have the opportunity to succeed or fail in your given responsibility.

A gatekeeper can be anyone who has the responsibility of opening the windows of Heaven to a city. They could be church leaders, intercessors, and every worshiper. An open heaven refers to the free access of God's presence to man and to the free flow of God's glory to man's dimension, with as little demonic hindrance as possible.

Lot was a gatekeeper in Sodom and Gomorrah. We know this because the Bible says Lot "sat in the gate of Sodom" (see Gen. 19:1). Despite his poor choice of cities, he clearly recognized righteousness when he encountered it in his angelic visitors. He specifically "opened the gates" to righteousness and welcomed his holy visitors into his home. Lot also recognized unrighteousness for what it was, but he failed to "close the gates" to the sin that was consuming his city. Because Lot didn't take the proper stand and have an effect on the city, Sodom and Gomorrah had an effect on him. In the end, *Sodom was destroyed by fire because God's gatekeeper didn't do his job.*

David also was a gatekeeper, but he understood the importance of his office. When he penned Psalm 84:10, I feel that he was saying, "I would rather be a doorkeeper at the right door, because that is the place of *real* influence." *Never underestimate the power of God's presence.* If you can be a doorkeeper and open the door of the manifest presence of God to your church and your community, understand that you have been placed in the most influential position in the entire world. Like the Levites of old, we are all called to be a gatekeeper people, the people of His presence. You can literally become a walking doorway to God's presence. People can sense the glory light shining under the door.

The man named Obededom discovered the importance of being a doorkeeper in the right place. Most believe that he was a part of the Levitical order, but we do know this much for sure about him: *He knew what it was like to have God dwell in his house instead of merely visit there.*

Obededom knew what to do when divine visitation turned into divine habitation, and he discovered there were side benefits that came with the job. His crops grew better, his dog stopped biting people, his roof didn't leak, his kids didn't get sick, and everything in his life was incredibly blessed. You know something good is going on when your crops are so blessed that, in three months time, everybody knows about it. Finally the word reached all the way to King David in Jerusalem: "David, you won't believe it: Obededom has turned into a millionaire in three months."

David said, "I knew I had it right. I've got to get that ark to Jerusalem. (See 2 Samuel 6:12.) If Obededom can be that blessed locally, then if I can put the ark in its proper place, we will all be blessed nationally."

Just how much was Israel blessed when David maintained the tabernacle all those years? Even though we haven't begun to worship and serve as we should, if the Church and its worship were withdrawn from the world today, things would spiral down very quickly. On the other hand, if the people of God can ever put the glory of God back in the Church in its proper place, the entire nation can be blessed.

Tommy Tenney – *God's Favorite House*

The Woman of Rejection Had an Appointment With Perfection

*J*esus probably watched the disciples pass the Samaritan woman in the road on their way to get food. (The disciples seemed to have a knack of missing momentous moments.) The woman who approached Jacob's well had been living a life of rejection. The Bible clearly tells us that she came at the noon hour (the sixth hour), and the women typically came in the morning to draw water for cooking and in the evening to draw water for bathing and washing. I think she wanted to avoid the biting remarks and judgmental stares of the women of the town.

Jesus saw past this woman's multiple husbands and saw the need of her heart. She admitted to having several husbands but made no mention of children. Perhaps this indicates that she was a barren woman who had no children. Is it possible that she went from husband to husband searching for someone to give her children? *Did she go through all that pain only to recognize in the end that the problem rested with her?*

As this woman walked up to Jacob's well, she probably thought she had run into something far worse than the sharp tongues of the townswomen—there was a Jewish rabbi waiting there. I can almost hear her thoughts: *He's probably a Pharisee who keeps every jot and tittle of the ancient law of Moses—including the requirement not to have any dealings with Samaritans.* Then the inconceivable happened: The Jewish holy man said, "I would like some water."

She expected to be rejected, but she wasn't prepared for Jesus' request. She said, "How can You ask me that? You are a Jew, and Jews aren't supposed to even speak to us." (See John 4:9.) In that moment, Jesus embarked on an intricate journey of leading a soul to a place of hunger by asking questions and making intriguing statements that drew her deeper into the conversation.

> *"If you knew the gift of God, and who it is who says to you, 'Give Me a drink,' you would have asked Him, and He would have given you living water." The woman said to Him, "Sir, You have nothing to draw with, and the well is deep. Where then do You get that living water?"* (John 4:10-11)

Jesus ultimately helped the woman understand that He wasn't talking about the kind of water found in Jacob's well. He was talking about living water and worship. He revealed the purpose for their divine appointment when He said,

> *"Woman, believe Me, the hour is coming when you will neither on this mountain, nor in Jerusalem, worship the Father.... But the hour is coming, and now is, when the **true worshipers** will worship the Father in spirit and truth; for **the Father is seeking such** to worship Him. God is Spirit, and those who worship Him must worship in spirit and truth"* (John 4:21-24).

That Samaritan woman had walked to Jacob's well with a thirst for well water, but she wound up meeting the Well of Life and discovered she was really thirsty for living water. Jesus told her, "The Father is seeking such to worship Him." The *only thing that the Father is actively seeking is worshipers!*

Tommy Tenney – *God's Favorite House*

The Anointing Is About Us; the Glory Is About Him

G od uses His anointing to train us, cleanse us, heal us, and prepare us for His manifest presence in ways reminiscent of the way the king's chamberlain prepared Esther for the king of Persia. In the end, the anointing takes us back to the altar of God and the place of repentance. Repentance, in turn, can usher in the very glory of God.

If you are anointed, you will preach better, pray better, minister better, and worship better and with greater freedom, but that is not His highest purpose. *The anointing is all about us, but the glory is all about Him.* The anointing refers to what He pours, smears, or places upon us to help us do His will. Sometimes it acts as a "perfume" to prepare us for intimacy, as in Esther's case. When the anointing of God rests on you, it makes whatever you do "better." It doesn't matter whether you preach, sing, witness, usher, pray, or minister to the babies in the back. When the anointing comes upon you, it empowers your gifts, talents, and callings with the power of God. Nevertheless, it is still the anointing, and it rests on flesh.

The glory is different. When the glory of God comes, you suddenly and clearly understand why God said "no flesh should glory in His presence" (1 Cor. 1:29). A more literal translation of this passage might be, "no flesh should glory in God's face." I can testify from personal experience and prove from the Scriptures that when the glory comes, your flesh can't do anything. Have you noticed that when people have a "God encounter" in the Bible, they usually end up on their face? *It is because they didn't really have a choice.*

The difference between the anointing of God and the glory of God is like the difference between the tiny blue spark of static electricity and the raw power of a 440-volt power line overhead or a lightning strike on your head! We are so busy rubbing our feet across the carpet of God's promises and giving one another tiny blue sparks of anointing that we don't realize God wants to jolt us with His 440-volt glory line from Heaven. The one will thrill you a little, but you get the feeling the other might kill you or change your life forever.

I love the anointing of God, and I am thankful for every good gift He has given us. Yet I am convinced God's first choice is for us to seek His face of favor rather than His hand of anointing. I've spent most of my life in church (multiple services up to five days per week since childhood). Personally, I've had enough anointed preaching and singing to last me two lifetimes. It's good and it's thrilling, but I must tell you the anointing in and of itself is not going to get the job done. *We must have the manifest presence of God Himself on display for the world.*

Failure to discern between the good and the best can cause us to make uneven trades. *Esther refused to trade the winking approval of men in the king's court for the favor of the king himself.* As a result, the king told Esther right in front of her enemy, "What is your petition? It shall be granted you. What is your request, up to half the kingdom? It shall be done!" (Esther 5:6b) *God is looking for a Bride-Church that has eyes only for Him.* Then He will delight in giving her the key to the city and the life of the nation.

Set your sights on the goal of breaking open the heavens to behold His glory over your city and nation. It is easy to mark the churches that have learned how to focus anointing vertically for God's favor instead of horizontally toward men.

Just look for the glory-filled footprints of God leading to their door.

They have had a visitation.

Tommy Tenney – *God's Favorite House*

"It Was Too Much of God"

Certain people throughout Church history have known about the glory. Smith Wigglesworth was certainly one who knew about it. In one of the biographies about his life, the story is told that a pastor began to pray with Wigglesworth, and he was determined to stay in the prayer room with him. In the end, he finally had to crawl out of the room on his hands and knees, saying, "It was too much of God." That is possible. You can walk at that place. Ask Enoch. The end result of this quest is that all that remains is God's glory, not man's anointed gifts, ministry, opinions, or abilities. In God's manifest presence, you and I will need to do very little, yet great and mighty things will happen. On the other hand, when you and I do "our thing," the results are few and there isn't much of God's glory in it. That's the difference.

Another illustration of the difference between the anointing and the glory is this: When you scrape your feet across the carpet on a fresh cold day and touch the tip of someone's nose, you will get a spark. You will also get a spark if you grab a 220-volt power line with your bare hands. In both cases, the power behind the spark is electricity and they both operate from the same principle. One will just give you a spark, but the other has the potential to instantly kill you or to light up your whole world. They both share the same source, but they differ in power, purpose, and scope.

If we allow God to replace our programs with His manifested presence, then whenever people walk through the doors of our local church building or when they mingle with us at the mall, they will be convicted of sin and could rush to get right with God without a word being spoken.

We need to learn how to entertain and welcome the manifested presence of God to such a degree that just the residue of what has gone on among us brings sinners to the point of conviction and conversion instantaneously. I am hungry for that kind of expression of revival, but if we're not careful we are going to let the lamp flicker out. We do not have a lock on God because we're not married to Him yet. He is still just looking for a bride without spot or wrinkle, and we need to remember that He already left one bride at the altar and He'll leave another.

I believe that God will literally destroy the Church *as we know it* if He has to so He can reach the cities. He is not in love with our imperfect versions of His perfect Church; He is only out to claim the house that *God built.* If our foul-smelling, man-made monstrosity stands in the way of what He wants to do, then He will move our junk pile aside to reach the hungry. His heart is to reach the lost, and if He spared not His own Son to save the lost, then He won't spare us either.

We must move into agreement with what God wants to do. The same Bible you and I carry to church services week after week says, "If we don't praise Him, then the rocks will cry out." (See Luke 19:40.) If the Church won't praise Him and obey Him, then He will raise up people who will. If we won't sing of God's glory in the streets of the cities, then He will raise up a generation that is nonreligious and uninhibited and reveal His glory to them. His problem is that we suffer from the spiritually fatal disease of reluctance. We're just not hungry enough!

Tommy Tenney – *The God Chasers*

When You Seek God's Glory, Things Get Heavier, Not Easier

*D*avid and his procession of Levites, priests, and worshipers paid a dear price to usher God's presence into their city that day. It is no wonder that when that crew finally arrived at the gate of Jerusalem, *David turned into a dancing, spinning fool!* Why? They were thankful they survived the trip! I think everyone in the procession was shouting, "We made it!" Any way you look at it, this was a bloody, smoky process.

I believe it will be the same for us today. Hear me, friend: When you move from the level of anointing to calling for the glory of God to come, things don't get easier. *They get heavier.*

Most people go for the new cart method because it represents a low-cost, no-sweat method of worship. God warned Adam and Eve at the beginning of their life outside the gates of Paradise, "You are going to live by the sweat of your brow" (see Gen. 3:19).

"Sweat" has particular significance to God. It is the means by which value is transferred on earth. In modern terms, if you want to transfer money from the boss's account to your back pocket, you will have to sweat or labor in some way. In the same way, farmers have to sweat if they want to transfer value from the soil into their bank account to feed their families.

It could be that you "sweat" out a report in an air-conditioned office. Or you might drench yourself with literal sweat driving nails at a construction site. David understood this and refused to offer to God *things* that came to him at no cost! (See 2 Samuel 24:24.) He would spend money he earned by sweating out the problems of the kingdom to purchase the ground and animals to sacrifice. He would also offer "sweaty" worship in the dance.

Sweat transfers value. It requires "sweat" to worship! Worship is actually "worth-ship," the transferring of value from us to God. That is why the giving of tithes and offerings are a part of worship. We transfer sweaty hours into dollars and then give sweaty money to God in an act of worship. This is just another way of transferring our "time" to Him. Whether you sweat figuratively or literally, you will sweat if you want to make a living. *And you will "sweat" if you really want to worship.*

When the flesh of our humanity gets lazy, we try to import or carry the things of God using no-sweat methods so we can walk along beside them and get all excited about "transporting the glory." The truth is that we don't want to sweat it out ourselves.

Tommy Tenney – *God's Favorite House*

Moving From Anointing to Glory

*"Do you quietly bow your head in reverence
when you step into the average church?
I would be surprised if your answer is yes."*
A.W. Tozer

My life changed forever on the October weekend in Houston, Texas, when God's presence invaded the atmosphere like a thunderbolt and split the podium at the Sunday service. I'll never forget telling my friend, the pastor, "You know, *God could have killed you.*" I wasn't laughing when I said it. It was as if God had said, "I'm here and I want you to *respect* My presence." A picture of Uzzah's grave had popped into my mind.

We didn't know what we were asking for when we said we "wanted God." I know I thought I did, but I didn't. When God actually showed up, none of us were prepared for the reality of His presence. As I've already mentioned earlier in this book, there was very little preaching because we didn't have a choice. God repossessed His church for a period of time and He wouldn't allow anything to happen that He hadn't specifically ordained for that service.

The thick blanket of His tangible presence was so heavy that I received an "up close and personal" understanding of what is meant by God's Word when it says:

*And it came to pass, when the priests were come out of the
holy place, that the cloud filled the house of the Lord,*

*So that the priests **could not stand to minister** because of
the cloud: for the glory of the Lord had filled the house of the
Lord* (1 Kings 8:10-11 KJV).

God came so suddenly and so forcefully into that church building that we were afraid to do anything unless He specifically told us
to do it. His presence was always there of course, but not the
weighty manifest presence we experienced at certain times. In those
moments, all we could do was sit there, trembling. We were afraid to
take an offering without specific permission from God. We kept asking each other, "Do you think it's okay to take an offering? Do you
think we should do this? What about that?"

Tommy Tenney – *The God Chasers*

This Is What Glory Does to the Flesh of Man

We all can agree that Jesus Christ shed His blood to take care of this sin problem. Yet in every instance where I have seen a measure of God's glory enter a worship service, *a godly reverence, fear, and dread of His glory also entered the room.* Even redeemed, blood-washed church leaders who lead holy lives suddenly feel a deep urgency to fall on their faces and repent before their holy God when His *kabod,* or weighty presence, begins to fill the room. This is what glory does to the flesh of man— even the flesh of the redeemed. This is why the earthy disciples always had to be reassured when a theophany or an angel appeared before them. *They feared that the glory would kill them!*

For this reason, God says to us with one hand, "Come close." Yet with the other hand He says, "Not so fast." It can be frightening to come too close to God's holy presence when there are specks of unrepented sin in your life. Yes, we are covered by the blood of Christ, but that doesn't release us from the felt need to repent of our sins and shortcomings anew when we encounter the holiness of His presence. Do we need to "get saved all over again"? Absolutely not! But do we often *feel* like "getting saved all over again"? Absolutely! Isaiah did! John did—he fell at His feet "as though dead"! (See Revelation 1:17.)

Jesus covers us with His blood to allow us to come into His presence in our unregenerated state. "What do you mean, unregenerated?"

We are not perfect, but we are living under the mantle of forgiveness—we are covered by the blood of the perfect sinless sacrifice—so we can enter in. That is where we're at now under the new covenant of Christ's blood, but somehow David stumbled across that same principle under the old covenants of Moses and the Old Testament when he began transporting the ark from Obededom's house. *It was a bloody, smoky process that led to David's wild dance through the gates of Jerusalem.*

What we are learning from his experience is that the repentant, brokenhearted nature of true worship only heightens the rich aroma of our acceptable sacrifice to God, and it is this offering that persuades the King of Glory to habitate with us instead of merely visit our meetings. When His glory finally comes through the gates of worship into our churches and cities, *we too might become dancing fools!*

There is no better way to wage spiritual warfare than to turn on the light of God's glory by ushering in His manifest presence. Allow Him to rebuild His favorite house in your gatherings and refuse to stop short at false finish lines or to be satisfied merely by the scent of where He once was.

Persist in your urgent longing for and pursuit of His presence and the heavens will open. His *shekinah* glory will descend on the mercy seat that your love and adoration have made just for Him. It is in this atmosphere of intimacy and devotion to God and God alone where His manifest presence shows up. When He turns on the light of His glory, demonic forces are instantly decimated. Captives are released and set free to run to their Redeemer just as the demoniac was released even before he met or heard Jesus speak.

When the heavens are open and God's light shines on the darkness, every demon and dark work is forced out because *the gates of hell can never prevail* or even put up a respectable fight when the very presence of the King of glory shows up. *Conduct spiritual warfare for your church and city in the same way God conducts it in Heaven* and you'll create a "DFZ" (a demon-free zone)! Pray and worship Him until the windows of Heaven open wide over your church and city. Worship Him until the light of His glory shines upon you.

"O Lord, on earth as it is in Heaven—show us Your glory!"

Tommy Tenney – *God's Favorite House*

The Burial of Man's Glory Is the Birth of God's Glory

We have lost the art of adoring the Lord. Our worship gets so cluttered with endless strings of shallow and insincere words that all we do most of the time is "take up space" or "put in prayer time" with a passionless monologue that even God must ignore.

Some of us come to Him clinging to such heavy burdens that we are too frustrated and distracted to see the Father or understand how much He loves us. We need to return to the simplicity of our childhood. Every night that I'm home, I rock my six-year-old daughter to sleep because I love her. Usually she will lay back in my arms, and just before she drifts off to sleep she will remember the problems of the day and say something like, "Daddy, this little boy was mean to me on the playground at school," or "Daddy, I had trouble on my spelling test today." To her these seem like giant problems. I always try to reassure her that everything will be all right in those moments because she is resting in my arms and because I love her. It doesn't matter what anyone said on the playground, and none of her little failures have any power to hurt her because she is in my arms.

Somehow, when I'm able to weave my way through the labyrinth of a six-year-old mind and bring peace to her, I get to enjoy my favorite part of the day. That is when my little girl just lays her head back to look at me with her eyes half open and give me her little smile. The only way I know to describe it is that her face displays sheer adoration and complete security in those moments. She doesn't have to speak; I understand. And then in complete peace she drifts off to sleep, with the smile of safety and trust on her face.

God wants us to do the same thing. Too often we come to Him at the end of our day and "worship" Him with premanufactured mechanics and memorized words. Then, since we are almost totally absorbed with our "playground" offenses and the temporal problems of the day, we lay back in His presence just long enough to say our string of words and deliver our wish list. Then we jump up and run off to continue our frustrated rat-race lives. Often we never seem to find that place of perfect peace.

What He wants us to do is just look at Him. Yes, we can tell Him what we feel. We need to tell Him, but He is really waiting to receive our most intimate worship and adoration, the kind that transcends mere words or outward actions. He has set before you an open door, but you will have to "face" Him. You cannot back your way into the door of eternity; you have to walk into it. You will have to stop looking at and listening to other things. He is beckoning to you to "come up hither," and He'll show you the "hereafter" (see Rev. 4:1). That should bring peace to a weary child.

Tommy Tenney – *The God Chasers*

Prop Open the Door So the King of Glory Can Come In

You have the keys in your hand, transferred by the Spirit through the leadership of the Church since Jesus first delivered them into Peter's hands. Are you going to unlock the windows of Heaven and lock up the gates of hell? Will you prop open the door so the King of Glory can personally come in to *rebuild His favorite house*, **the house that worship built**?

In the meantime, God is peeping out through the mini-blinds of Heaven and saying, "I want to throw open the window. I want to do away with the veil. I've hated veils from the beginning, so I rip them every time I get a chance. If I can get the Church to take its place as repentant worshipers around the throne, I will throw open the windows of Heaven. *Judgment will stop with My worshipers, but My mercy will slip through to the pagans and heathens looking in at the Church.*" They won't even see the worshipers because their backs are turned to the world. All they will see is the blue flame of the *shekinah* glory of God. And the lost will say, "That's mercy." That's the mercy seat.

God is still hiding from the world because He cannot flow through the streets until the Church takes its place and begins to filter the glory. So the hunting eyes of God are darting to and fro while He asks, "Where is somebody who will be a go-between, who will stand in the gap and make up the hedge? Don't let it fall. Hold it high for other places and other people. I'm looking for somebody who can prop open the windows of Heaven in the weeping zone."

With this revelation there comes responsibility. Don't expect to go about business as usual because you now know where the Church is supposed to stand. It is okay to be seeker-friendly, but our first calling is to be Spirit-friendly. *Seeker-friendly is fine, but Spirit-friendly is fire!* We must let our Uzzahs die so the glory can be restored to God as we reach for Heaven with one hand and the earth with the other.

Can you feel the wind and the breeze of the Spirit whipping between your legs? When God shows up in your services, it is better than having billboards around town. Services like that do more than any TV advertisement. Why? Because it doesn't attract man; it attracts God. If you get God, then you don't have to worry about man. The hungry will come.

If you can just learn how to stand in a place like that, you will begin to feel surrounded by His presence. As you begin to walk in it, your life becomes a walking window of His presence that is subject to being opened at any time by soul-hungry men. That means that the glory of God could break out every time you visit a grocery store or a convenience store.

Something is shaking the Church. We hit a bump, our new cart was shaken, and our Uzzahs are dying or dead. We want Him, but we've had to learn the right ways to welcome and reverence His presence. Our shaking hands have found the rip in the veil. We've found the door of Heaven, and God is looking for a place of habitation. Throw open the veil and keep it open. *One good service is not enough.*

Tommy Tenney – *God's Favorite House*

Take a Stand Between the Glory and Sinful Men

A plague of sin and death is sweeping across our nation and the world today. This is no time to run or hide. This is the time for you and me to enter the weeping zone with our priestly censers of worship and take our stand between the living and the dead, between the weighty glory of God and the unprotected flesh of sinful men. The moment Aaron carried the coals from the fire of the altar and mixed in the incense of worship and prayer, he became a bridge between two worlds.

God has a heart to see all men saved, but He depends on you and me to fulfill our ministry of reconciliation in the weeping zone. He has called us to become bridges between the kingdom of light and the kingdom of darkness. The greatest Bridge of all is Jesus Christ, our great High Priest who ever lives to intercede for us before the Father. (See Hebrews 7:25.) When you and I enter the weeping zone, we come alongside the Great Intercessor and face the throne, reaching out for God with one hand and for man with the other. We are called to intercede in worship until God and man have met together.

When you stand in the gap, you are literally stopping the judgment of God and moving aside the obstacles of the enemy in the second heaven. As we noted earlier, John said, "We beheld His glory...full of grace and truth" (Jn. 1:14b).

If the two components of God's glory are grace and truth, then that explains why there always had to be a veil separating man from God's glory. *The world needs God's grace, but His truth is attached to it.* The truth is, we have all sinned and come short of the glory of God (see Rom. 3:23). We need His grace—but we can't stand the "truth." His truth is equivalent to His *judgment,* and apart from God's grace through Jesus Christ, none of us have a chance. That means that if God's manifest presence—the thing we are praying for—rushes out and encounters unrepentant flesh, then the truth or judgment of God will instantly obliterate it just as light obliterates darkness.

If you really want an outbreak of the glory of God in your church and city, you will have to forget about what anybody else except God thinks. Real revival happens only when true worshipers forget about man and turn their full attention and adoration toward God. We must forget about the opinions and approval or disapproval of people. We need to forget what they look like, forget what they are saying, and forget what they are thinking. *Only one opinion matters.*

I wish that God's people would ignore everything but what God wants. It is time for the centrality of Christ Jesus to so overwhelm and overpower us that we become totally disconnected from the distractions of the realm of man. I'm not talking about becoming so religious that we are absolutely no good to God or man. Some people say that you can become so heavenly minded that you are no earthly good, but I'm not sure that is possible. In fact, that phrase is a good description of the "weeping zone," that place between the porch of man and the altar of God. Can I tell you what you do in that position? *The weeping zone is the place of intercession before God's throne* where you step into the gap to intercede for others.

Tommy Tenney – *God's Favorite House*

The Next Wave of Glory

I believe that some cities are old wells of God's anointing—places of historical revival. God is calling pastors and congregations in those cities to redig those wells. Unfortunately, digging the debris out of an old well is not a pleasant task. When a pastor friend of mine bought some property in India, he was told that there was an old well on the property. It wasn't a common "vertical" well; it was slanted horizontally into the side of a mountain.

As the ministry workers began to dig out the debris, they found old machinery, discarded furniture, and mounds of old trash among high stands of overgrown weeds and rushes. They found something else too: They encountered hundreds of cobras in that abandoned well, and they had to be removed. My friend told me, "We got that old well all cleaned out and went to bed. When we got up the next morning, we hoped and expected to find a pool of stagnant water waiting for us. But we discovered that the water in the well had begun to bubble up and was flowing so strongly again that it had created a stream overnight!"

The next wave will come as God uncaps the artesian wells of His glory! Many of the wells in the deserts of the Middle East are "standing pool wells." There is enough water seeping up into the natural holding tank of the earth to keep it filled most of the time, even in the desert heat. Almost every living thing in the desert ecosystem makes its way to the oasis or standing pool well for the water of life. God has uncapped abundant standing pools of His presence that have brought life to millions of thirsty believers and unsaved people over the last few years. But they must travel to the well. There is forgotten power in pilgrimage.

Now He is about to release the next stage or wave of His anointing, and it will be unlike the old standing pool wells in that these new wells will be *artesian wells* that will explode with great force. According to *Webster's Ninth New Collegiate Dictionary*, an "artesian well" is "a well made by boring into the earth until water is reached *which from internal pressure flows up like a fountain*; a *deep-bored well*" (*Webster's Ninth New Collegiate Dictionary* [Springfield, MA: Merriam-Webster, Inc., 1988], 105). This new wave or level of God's glory will come solely from the "deep-bored" people of God's presence. It will explode into our world with such force that His life-giving presence will push beyond every barrier and obstacle to flow into the thirsty streets of our cities and nations. This is how His glory will "cover the whole earth" (see Is. 6:3; Hab. 2:14). Fountains of the deep will break open!

You don't have to go to the waters of an artesian well; *the water goes to you!* Given the fact that water always seeks the lowest level and the path of least resistance, it is easy to see why Jesus, the "brightness of [the Father's] glory, and the express image of His person" (Heb. 1:3a), said, "...the poor have the gospel preached to them" (Mt. 11:5). God's glory always seeks to fill the void in the lives of men. In the days to come, God's glory will emanate from the most confounding places and individuals, and it will begin to flow and fill the lowest and most open of people. And He alone will receive the glory.

Tommy Tenney – *The God Chasers*

Anointing to Glory

My youngest daughter, Andrea, recently got a shiny new bike. She saved her allowance and paid for half of the purchase. She could hardly contain her excitement! Anybody who came anywhere near the house would be temporarily detained while she proudly described its finer features. A little bike is a big deal to a girl Andrea's age, and I can't help but smile when I see her ear-to-ear, missing-tooth grin.

I treasure these moments with my daughters...children grow up so quickly! Sometimes they grow so quickly that we don't even realize how big they've gotten. Andrea's affections have only recently transferred to her two-wheeler. Her former love (which still resides in our garage!) was a battery-powered Barbie Jeep. Surely you've seen them: big pink plastic wheels, pink and white plastic body, plastic seat, rechargeable battery capable of propelling child and toy at the staggering velocity of 3 to 4 miles per hour...it was Andrea's favorite toy. She wore the thing out!

That plastic car received more repairs in less time than any vehicle in the Tenney family history. We probably spent more on replacement parts than we did on the original purchase! The bigger she got, the more often it would break—not because of the age of the toy as much as the age of the child. It just wasn't designed for children her age, and no amount of repair could alter that fundamental fact. This sort of reasoning is readily apparent to an adult, but try to explain that to a frustrated seven-year-old who can't fit in the seat and has to sit on the trunk—and wedge her feet into position to make it go!

Do you have any Barbie cars in your garage? It might not be a pathetic pink plastic plaything, but if you look hard enough you'll probably discover some relics of your own—things in your spiritual garage that used to work but no longer seem to do the job. Maybe you've been scratching your head wondering why that music or that favorite preacher or program no longer ushers you into the presence of God like it used to. There comes a time when the things that were once "tried and true" are now "tired and blue."

King David found himself in that position when he tried to move the ark of the covenant to Jerusalem. The Philistines had sent the ark back to Israel on a cart, so when David wanted to bring it home, he probably didn't think twice about how he transported it. After all, a cart worked before...why not use it again?

David gathered together all the chosen men of Israel, thirty thousand....And David and all the house of Israel played before the Lord on all manner of instruments made of fir wood, even on harps, and on psalteries, and on timbrels, and on cornets, and on cymbals (2 Samuel 6:1,5).

It wasn't even an old cart—that wouldn't do! It was a new cart. Only the best for God! The celebration upon the ark's arrival in Jerusalem would be spectacular! And it would all begin with a grand procession...David and all his best men leading the parade.

GodChasers.network newsletter

Are You Going to Let Him Get Close?

I believe that this generation is very close to revival, but I don't want to simply watch as God passes down the street to go somewhere else where people really *want Him.* "It's going to happen *somewhere,* but if not us, *who,* Lord? We aren't satisfied with Your gifts, as wonderful as they are. We want You." The equation for revival is still the same:

> *If My people, which are called by My name,* **shall humble themselves** *[die on the altar of repentance], and pray,* **and seek My face** *[instead of just revival or momentary visitations], and turn from their wicked ways; then will I hear from heaven, and will forgive their sin, and will heal their land* (2 Chronicles 7:14 KJV).

"Father, we seek Your face."

As God redefines the Church, it is highly likely that the Church that emerges from the cloud of His glory will look very different from what you and I think the Church should look like. This will happen because God is repossessing the Church and drawing it close to Him.

Will we dare to draw close to His glory? God really wanted the children of Israel to come up and receive the Ten Commandments directly from Him along with Moses. But they ran from God's presence. The Church is in danger of doing the same thing today. We can take the risk of something dying in us as we dare to draw close to His glory, or we can turn and run back to our traditions of men and the safety of religious legalism and man-operated church services. *Seeker-friendly is fine; Spirit-friendly is fire!*

Let's create a comfort zone for God and a discomfort zone for man by repentant worship. Our churches are more comfortable for man, plush with padding, than they are comfortable for God, stripped of flesh!

The Israelites literally isolated and insulated themselves from God's intimate presence because of their fear of death. Moses, on the other hand, drew near to the thick darkness concealing God's glory. It is time for the Church to truly embrace the cross of Jesus. Our hunger must propel us beyond the death of the flesh into the life and light of God's glory. It is the destiny of the Church of the living God. But it will only happen when we lay down the security of the "new covenant law" of religious practice and carefully controlled "supernatural" visitations for the apparent uncertainty and risk of living face to face with our supernatural God.

God doesn't want us to turn away from His glory so we can build pitiful monuments to a momentary revelation we never paid for with our tears. *Salvation is a free gift, but God's glory will cost us everything.* He wants us to press in and *live* in His perpetual habitation of glory. He wants us to be so saturated with His presence and glory that we carry His presence with us everywhere we go in this life. This may be the only way the unspeakable glory of God will find its way to the shopping malls, hair style salons, and grocery stores of our nation.

This is the way God's glory is destined to cover the whole earth. It has to start somewhere. The fountains of flesh have to be broken up, as well as the windows of Heaven opened up, for the glory to begin to flow like a river and cover the earth. Jesus said, "Out of [your] belly shall flow rivers of living water" (Jn. 7:38b). We will have to be totally sold out to Him if His glory is going to cover the earth.

The difference between the anointing and the glory is the difference between God's hands and His face, and the path to the glory of God takes us right up to the altar where we must lay everything down and die. In the end, we will find ourselves face to face with God as a nation of "dead men walking," in possession of His glory. Nothing else is needed; nothing else is necessary. Once God's children lay down their toys and crawl into the Father's lap to seek His face, the House of Bread will once again overflow with fresh bread and every good gift. *The hungry will find the eternal satisfaction that they've always longed for.*

He will not frustrate us. God will allow Himself to be caught by us. As a father playing tag with his child allows himself to be caught by the laughing, loving child, so too will the heavenly Father allow Himself to be caught. In fact, just when you would tire in despair, He will turn and catch you. He wants to be "captured" by our love. He eagerly awaits the laughing, loving encounter. He has missed those times with man since the Garden. Intuitively, God chasers have known this. *They were willing to chase the "uncatchable," knowing the "impossible" would catch them.* In fact, one famous God chaser wrote this:

> ***I follow after, if that I may apprehend*** *that for which also I am apprehended of Christ Jesus* (Philippians 3:12b KJV).

Paul caught Him!

So can you! Come join the company of God chasers!

The "chase" is on....

Tommy Tenney – *Extreme GodChasers*

GODChasers.network

GodChasers.network is the ministry of Tommy and Jeannie Tenney. Their heart's desire is to see the presence and power of God fall—not just in churches, but on cities and communities all over the world.

How to contact us:

By Mail:

GodChasers.network
P.O. Box 3355
Pineville, Louisiana 71361
USA

By Phone:

Voice:	318.44CHASE (318.442.4273)
Fax:	318.442.6884
Orders:	888.433.3355

By Internet:

E-mail:	GodChaser@GodChasers.net
Website:	www.GodChasers.net

Join Today

When you join the **GodChasers.network** we'll send you a free teaching tape!

If you share in our vision and want to stay current on how the Lord is using GodChasers.network, please add your name to our mailing list. We'd like to keep you updated on what the Spirit is saying through Tommy. We'll also send schedule updates and make you aware of new resources as they become available.

Sign up by calling or writing to:

Tommy Tenney
GodChasers.network
P.O. Box 3355
Pineville, Louisiana 71361-3355
USA

318-44CHASE (318.442.4273)
or sign up online at http://www.GodChasers.net/lists/

We regret that we are only able to send regular postal mailings to certain countries at this time. If you live outside the U.S. you can still add your postal address to our mailing list—you will automatically begin to receive our mailings as soon as they are available in your area.

E-mail Announcement List

If you'd like to receive information from us via e-mail, just provide an e-mail address when you contact us and let us know that you want to be included on the e-mail announcement list!

BOOKS BY

THE GOD CHASERS
$12.00 plus $4.50 S&H

What is a God Chaser? A person whose hunger exceeds his reach ... a person whose passion for God's presence presses him to chase the impossible in hopes that the uncatchable might catch him.

The great God Chasers of the Scripture, Moses, Daniel, David—see how they were driven by hunger born of tasting His goodness. They had seen the invisible and nothing else satisfied. Add your name to the list. Come join the ranks of the God Chasers.

CHASING GOD, SERVING MAN
$17.00 plus $4.50 S&H

Using the backdrop of Bethany and the house of Mary and Martha, Tommy Tenney biblically explores new territory. The revolutionary concepts in this book can change your life. You will discover who you really are! (and unlock the secret of who "they" really are!)

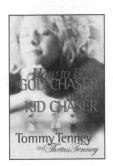

HOW TO BE A GODCHASER AND A KID CHASER
$12.00 plus $4.50 S&H

Combining years of both spiritual passion and practical parenting, Tommy Tenney and his mother, Thetus Tenney, answer the questions that every parent has. Helping them are the touching and sometimes humorous insights of such Christian greats as Dutch and Ceci Sheets, Cindy Jacobs and others. You'll have to open this book to discover.

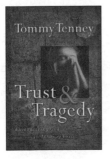

TRUST AND TRAGEDY
$7.00 plus $4.50 S&H

When tragedy strikes, your desperate hunt for hope in the secular forest will be futile. The hunters invariably go home empty-handed and brokenhearted, because humanity doesn't have the answers. Jesus gave us the key in one of the most direct and unequivocal statements ever made: "I am the way, the truth, and the life. No one comes to the Father, except through me." This book is a signpost along the way, through the truth, and to the life. If life is what you need, trust in God will take you there.

VIDEOTAPE ALBUMS BY

Tommy Tenney

GOING HOME FROM A FUNERAL
Video $20.00 $10.00 plus $4.50 S&H

Our country is now in a crisis. Some things will never be the same. Our national mentality is as if we are "going home from a funeral." We are no longer in the orderly, controlled funeral procession. Cars have scattered, taking their own routes back to individual homes and routines. The lights are off and reality hits.

FOLLOW THE MAN ON THE COLT
Video $20.00 plus $4.50 S&H

From humility to authority.... If we learn to ride the colt of humility, then we qualify to ride on the stallion of authority.

(This new video helps us understand that we all start this journey crawling—which strengththens us to walk—that empowers us to run—and rewards us to ride!) Enjoy this great teaching by Tommy Tenney on following the Man on the colt. It will change the way you see the obstacles put in your path! Remember, there is never a testimony without a test!

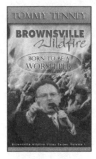

BROWNSVILLE WILDFIRE SERIES, VOL. 1
"Born to Be a Worshiper"
Video $20.00 plus $4.50 S&H

God would rather hear the passionate praises of His children than the perfection of heavenly worship. It isn't about how good we are as singers, or how skilled we are as musicians. It isn't about singing catchy choruses with clever words. It's all about GOD, and if we'll let our guard down and allow ourselves to truly worship Him, we'll find that He's closer than we ever imagined. If you've been born into God's kingdom, then you were born to be a worshiper! It's time to do the very thing that we were created for!

TURNING ON THE LIGHT OF THE GLORY
Video $20.00 plus $4.50 S&H

Tommy deals with turning on the light of the glory and presence of God, and he walks us through the necessary process and ingredients to potentially unleash what His Body has always dreamed of.

AUDIOTAPE ALBUMS BY

WHAT'S THE FIGHT ABOUT?
(audiotape album) $20 plus $4.50 S&H

Tape 1 — Preserving the Family: God's special gift to the world is the family! If we don't preserve the family, the church is one generation from extinction. God's desire is to heal the wounds of the family from the inside out.

Tape 2 — Unity in the Body: An examination of the levels of unity that must be respected and achieved before "Father let them be one" becomes an answered prayer!

Tape 3 — "IF you're throwing dirt, you're just losing ground!" In "What's the Fight About?" Tommy invades our backyards to help us discover our differences are not so different after all!

FANNING THE FLAMES
(audiotape album) $20 plus $4.50 S&H

Tape 1 — The Application of the Blood and the Ark of the Covenant: Most of the churches in America today dwell in an outer-court experience. Jesus made atonement with His own blood, once and for all, and the veil in the temple was rent from top to bottom.

Tape 2 — A Tale of Two Cities—Nazareth & Nineveh: What city is more likely to experience revival: Nazareth or Nineveh? You might be surprised....

Tape 3 — The "I" Factor: Examine the difference between *ikabod* and *kabod* ("glory"). The arm of flesh cannot achieve what needs to be done. God doesn't need us; we need Him.

KEYS TO LIVING THE REVIVED LIFE
(audiotape album) $20 plus $4.50 S&H

Tape 1 — Fear Not: To have no fear is to have faith, and perfect love casts out fear, so we must establish the trust of a child in our loving Father.

Tape 2 — Hanging in There: Have you ever been tempted to give up, quit, and throw in the towel? This message is a word of encouragement for you.

Tape 3 — Fire of God: Fire purges the sewer of our souls and destroys the hidden things that would cause disease. Learn the way out of a repetitive cycle of seasonal times of failure.

PURSUING HIS PRESENCE
(audiotape album) $20 plus $4.50 S&H

Tape 1 — Transporting the Glory: There comes a time when God wants us to grow to another level of maturity. For us, that means walking by the Spirit rather than according to the flesh.

Tape 2 — Turning on the Light of the Glory: Tommy walks us through the process of unleashing what the Body of Christ has always dreamed of: getting to the Glory!

Tape 3 — Building a Mercy Seat: In worship, we create an appropriate environment in which the presence of God can dwell. The focus of the church needs to be shifted from simply dusting the furniture to building the mercy seat.

Run With Us!

Become a GodChasers.network Monthly Revival Partner

Two men, a farmer and his friend, were looking out over the farmer's fields one afternoon. It was a beautiful sight—it was nearly harvest time, and the wheat was swaying gently in the wind. Inspired by this idyllic scene, the friend said, "Look at God's provision!" The farmer replied, "You should have seen it when God had it by Himself!"

This humorous story illustrates a serious truth. Every good and perfect gift comes from Him: but we are supposed to be more than just passive recipients of His grace and blessings. We must never forget that only God can cause a plant to grow—but it is equally important to remember that *we are called to do our part in the sowing, watering, and harvesting.*

When you sow seed into this ministry, you help us reach people and places you could never imagine. The faithful support of individuals like you allows us to send resources, free of charge, to many who would otherwise be unable to obtain them. Your gifts help us carry the gospel all over the world—including countries that have been closed to evangelism. Would you prayerfully consider partnering with us? As a small token of our gratitude, our Revival Partners who send a monthly gift of $20 or more receive a teaching tape every month. This ministry could not survive without the faithful support of partners like you!

Stand with me now—so we can run together later!

In Pursuit,

Tommy Tenney

Tommy Tenney

**Become a Monthly Revival Partner
by calling or writing to:**

Tommy Tenney/GodChasers.network

**P.O. Box 3355
Pineville, Louisiana 71361-3355
318.44CHASE (318.442.4273)**